REA

D1305722

POLO

Tommy Hitchcock in white with the ball,
backed up by J. Watson Webb, c. 1927

POLO

THE EMPEROR OF GAMES

FRANK MILBURN

Alfred A. Knopf   New York   1994

This is a Borzoi Book published by Alfred A. Knopf, Inc.

Copyright © 1994 by Frank Milburn
All rights reserved under International and Pan-American
Copyright Conventions. Published in the United States by
Alfred A. Knopf, Inc., New York, and simultaneously in Canada
by Random House of Canada Limited, Toronto. Distributed
by Random House, Inc., New York.

Library of Congress Cataloging-in-Publication Data
Milburn, Frank.
Polo: the emperor of games / Frank Milburn. — 1st ed.
p.   cm.
Includes index.
ISBN 0-394-57161-4
1. Polo—United States—History.   2. Polo—History.   I. Title.
GV1011.6.U6M55   1994
796.35'3—dc20   93-5157   CIP

Designed by Anthea Lingeman
Manufactured in the United States of America
FIRST EDITION

To Maria, Elizabeth, and Alexandra

POLO

Prologue

T HERE IS POLO, and then there is polo. In "polo" people say "chukker" and look swell. Polo is an entirely different matter. Winston Churchill called it "the emperor of games."

Polo combines all games played with a ball into one, with the addition of a horse. (Throughout this book I frequently use "horse" instead of "pony." Players have not used real ponies since 1900.) At its best, polo is a thrilling sport, perhaps the most thrilling. At its worst, nothing happens, and the nothing that happens takes a long time.

The expense can't be ignored. A newspaperman once asked Tommy Hitchcock—an American and one of the two best players who ever lived (the other being Juan Carlos Harriott of Argentina)—what went first in a mature polo player. He doubtless expected the great man to mention legs, eyes, or reflexes: things that go in mature athletes in other sports.

With typical bluntness, Hitchcock replied, "The money."

Polo is excellent for people who need to ostentate. There are fields and horses and grooms, vans, lovely parties—champagne companies often sponsor games—and one's own expensive team. Horses sell for up to $50,000. In 1989 an Australian industrialist offered $300,000 for La Luna, a horse owned by Gonzalo Pieres, the best active polo player in the world.

Polo is not vascular surgery, and the horse is 70 percent of the game.

Unfortunately, there is nothing quite like polo to get people going. The sport gives off vibrations, whether from Ralph Lauren models with thick hair or from playboys. Polo irritates people in a way that other sports don't. One reason may be the subtle sense emanated of a private game in which spectators are not so much welcomed as endured.

In polo one can point to the money—professional money, money for upkeep of the manicured field, money for boots and saddles, grooms, stables, and of course money for horses. That Australian who proposed $300,000 for a horse was not a master of the game. Unless a rider can match a horse's excellence, the horse will decline.

I know of Tommy Hitchcock only from historical records and eyewitnesses. It is generally believed that Scott Fitzgerald used him as a model for Tom Buchanan in *The Great Gatsby*, though there is no conclusive evidence of this.

Hitchcock was not universally beloved. There is one prominent American family—almost as prominent as the Rockefellers, Astors, or Vanderbilts—whose members played polo with and against Hitchcock in the 1920s and 1930s. They so loathed him that a half century after his death, and fully sixty years after his best playing days, the mere mention of his name provokes outbursts uncharacteristic of persons who make a gospel out of restraint. Hitchcock is still very much alive to them, and they never tire of rehashing old matches. They insist he was too hard on his horses, asserting that one afternoon he pulled up a horse and broke its back. The horse was dead before it hit the ground.

What really bothers them is that one day this family's top player loaned Hitchcock his best horse. When Tommy returned the animal, it had a bloody mouth. As Hitchcock strode away, he said, "That horse is no damn good."

The family never forgave him for that. A myth grew from twisted roots and became part of the family's iconography, passed down from generation to generation, animating even the oldest members, wheelchaired and be-caned. Hitchcock was a symbol to them of Bunyanesque brute strength, primitive zeal, unleashed forces of nature—something wild and untamed entering the old gentleman's game.

I asked my father, Devereux Milburn, Jr., who goes back a long way in polo, if the back-breaking incident was true. I deliberately phrased the question provocatively: "Did you know that Tommy Hitchcock once pulled up a horse and broke its back?"

The question stirred him. "Goddammit," he said.

He had rarely spoken about polo since retiring from the game in the late 1950s. He was a good player and for a long time had served as chairman of the U.S. Polo Association. He was president of the Meadow Brook Club on Long Island, the cradle of American polo, for forty-one years.

"I hope you're not going to publish that story," he added.

"Why not?" I asked innocently. "It's a good story."

"Tommy never broke a horse's back in his life. X [the patriarch of the family] made it up because he was mad that Tommy didn't like his horse."

Hitchcock is synonymous with polo and a vanished period in American life—the post–World War I flexings of a new global power. Even people who have never seen a polo game and never intend to have heard of him. He is trapped inside the last American era of unvarnished celebrity, along with Dempsey and Tunney, Big Bill Tilden, Bobby Jones, Babe Ruth, the Four Horsemen of Notre Dame. An era when American sports burst at the seams with heroes.

Now scarcely an American athlete escapes untarnished. Athletes often write books to explain how tarnished they are. They gamble; they keep mistresses; they can't stay away from drugs; they get caught carrying concealed weapons.

I was too young to see Hitchcock play, though sometimes it feels as if I did see him, since his family and mine were linked by polo for a long time.

In 1966 I did have the privilege of watching Juan Carlos Harriott, Hitchcock's coequal in greatness, play a championship match in Argentina against an American team. Harriott formed his own gravitational field and had a most lordly playing style, as if he had descended from mythical upper reaches just for the afternoon.

Everything about him was smooth and effortless; every shot placed. He rode less than he glided. He dominated the field arrayed and had a knack for bringing out the best classical play from both teams. I couldn't take my eyes off him.

He wrote, "A polo player must love his horse."

In nothing I've read about the game have I heard another player express this sentiment. For most, a horse is a vehicle, the faster the better. It gets him to the ball. If it can't get him to the ball, it is replaced.

POLO PERMITS nothing except its moment. It does not allow the heavy nostalgias of baseball, or invite literary meditations, though polo is about death, a writer's best topic. Death horrific; death right in front of the viewer; death with the viewer as participant; death narrowly avoided; death of horses in a machine age, giving the sport a grotesque hold on anachronism. Death plain. A polo player can wear no pad or garment to protect himself. There are new designs of helmets, but they often do more harm than good, slicing up the face like a wildly wielded scalpel.

Every few games something terrible happens; someone has an escape or doesn't. When a half-ton animal makes a miscue—slips, collides, or is thrown off balance—anything can happen. Because the game is so fast—and because a player is always inside distending surges of adrenaline—an accident gets compounded. Inferior players tend to reach for the unreachable, causing them to take flight from the security of their horses. They hang out there as flutteringly as a leaf. That is when they find themselves in mortal trouble. Sometimes they become the arc of a pendulum and either smash into the grass or are saved.

Polo has inspired almost no Western literature. Some early Churchill, a little Kipling (his book *The Maltese Cat* is fine), a mention by Edith Wharton, a hint from Scott Fitzgerald, and that's it.

Ernest Hemingway would have loved Tommy Hitchcock, so suited to his lean, clean, violent style. Hemingway was good friends with the poloists and sportsmen Raymond and Winston Guest, but I can find no record that he ever saw a game. Winston Guest played on several American international teams. Hemingway biographer Jeffrey Meyers wrote that Guest had the advantage from Hemingway's point of view of being genial, rich, and dim.

With its attractions of the high life, artistry, and grace, polo might appeal to writers, especially those who enjoy a champagne cossetting at sporting venues (which is just about all of us). But polo lacks the common touch, is off-putting, and what off-puts quickly annoys.

By contrast, thoroughbred horse racing—for me, a less interesting sport—and its array of colorful low-lifes has captured writers as diverse as Hemingway, Red Smith, Dick Francis, Bill Barich, Leo Tolstoy, and Damon Runyon. Every racetrack has stoopers and punters and exercise girls, pithy jockeys, vocal fans, witty trainers, crude or classy owners, and a long time between races to absorb booze. The Hialeah racetrack in Florida even had pink flamingos.

Contrasts of manure and cologne make literature. Hemingway at Auteuil, old money and new, camel's hair and polyester.

A race lasting two minutes or less is not nearly as interesting as a polo game, where horses go full speed and stop on a dime and then turn and gallop directly the other way. A horse has to aggressively want to close on an opponent's mount at full speed or is no good for polo. These qualities can almost be humanized.

It is hard to hit a small, bouncing white ball ninety yards at thirty-five miles per hour from four feet off the turf with a thin bamboo shaft attached to a mallet head one inch in diameter. Hit the ball frontways, sideways, backways, under the neck; or chip, slice, pass it far upfield onto another mallet, all the while coordinating the horse's gait and maintaining your own seat in the saddle.

Polo should have had a literary moment. There seemed a chance in the 1920s, when money was fast and a public hungry for stars coincided with a flowering of excellent sportswriting from Ring Lardner, Heywood Broun, and others.

No other sport played worldwide—from Zimbabwe to Queensland, from Argentina to British Columbia—has had so little effective prose written about it, even though conditions and players vary tremendously from one country to another.

(The best sports book ever written, C.L.R. James's *Beyond a Boundary*, is about cricket, so an elitist tinge does not necessarily interfere with good prose.)

As one example of colorful playing conditions, there is the tiny country of Brunei, situated on the island of Borneo in the South China Sea. It is ruled by the world's richest man, the sultan of Brunei, an avid poloist. His horses live in air-conditioned stables; otherwise, they would sweat to death. The thermometer climbs to more than 120 degrees daily with 100 percent humidity. Polo games in Brunei are torpid affairs, played under blanketing layers of tangible air.

There is another reason, more difficult to pinpoint, that polo did not offer itself as literature. Churchill and Kipling wrote of a society defined as clearly as the Gobi sun. They had no need to arrange details of background, because the imperial experience was familiar to every reader. By the same token, Edith Wharton had her cohesive background, Scott Fitzgerald his.

These societies have not existed for more than fifty years.

MANY YEARS AGO I saw a photograph, doctored and retouched to a fine mist of romantic reverence, of Man o' War, the great racehorse of the early 1920s. In the photograph he is held lovingly by his black groom as both ascend into heaven, levitating toward the beckoning clouds.

Modern realities are far different, but still we watch sports—to see who wins, who loses, who bears up or doesn't. Mostly, we wait for a surpassing moment when the grave odds of life are reversed; when time is either stopped or transfigured. We love these transfigurations. Shining performances are privileges granted only a few times in a life, and we will put up with anything to see them.

Part One

International Polo Cup, Hurlingham, 1921

Chapter One

HIS FRIENDS called him Dickie, but his full name was Louis Francis Albert Victor Nicholas Battenberg, or His Serene Highness Prince Louis of Battenberg. To avoid a German taint in World War I, his father changed the family surname to Mountbatten.

He was the great-grandson of Queen Victoria, the nephew of the czar and czarina of Russia, and a cousin of the king of England. He never let anyone forget his royal connections. As a naval officer—and self-admittedly a terrible sailor—promoted to successively higher posts, and finally to first sea lord, he held meetings in which his aides wagered privately on how often he would mention "my niece, the Queen," or "dear Lilibet."

He was a man of such astonishing vanity that Noel Coward might have dropped him whole into one of his brittle comedies. His sole reading matter throughout his life consisted of books on his own genealogy.

"A perfect example of British imperialism," declared Jawaharlal Nehru following their first meeting in 1947, after Mountbatten had been sent out as the last British viceroy to supervise India's partition and independence.

By 1947 India's illusory colonial order had collapsed. From London, Winston Churchill fumed about "half-naked fakirs," meaning Gandhi. The

Mahatma's nonviolent packaging—sandals, shepherd's staff, spinning-jenny, fasting—had no appeal for an aged warrior who in his youth had been thrilled to participate in the world's last great cavalry charge at Omdurman, so reminiscent of Kipling's savage lines in "The Young British Soldier" about another battle:

> *When you're wounded and left on Afghanistan's plains,*
> *And the women come out to cut up what remains,*
> *Jest roll to your rifle and blow out your brains*
> *An' go to your Gawd like a soldier.*

Half-bagged by sunset and rarely awake before ten in the morning, Churchill on the surface had less in common with Gandhi than with any man on earth, but more in common than he cared to acknowledge. Driving ambition, of course, and the heroic strength to do things his way or the motorway.

Gandhi drove Churchill to distraction. "I hate Indians," declared the toothless lion. "They are a beastly people with a beastly religion." (He had said of the 1935 Government of India Act: "A monstrous monument of shame built by pigmies.")

Half a century before, the twenty-two-year-old Churchill had lounged under canvas at Bangalore, organizing his polo team for the regimental championships. India was halcyon then, a colony where Churchill, the son of a syphilitic lord (who was himself the noninheriting younger son of a duke) and a fortune-squandering American nymphomaniac could make his mark.

India was a world away from musketry training at Sandhurst, the military college from where, lonely and penniless, Churchill had written his parents a desolating cri de coeur: "I am cursed with so feeble a body that I can hardly support the fatigues of the day...."

.   .   .

ON SEPTEMBER 11, 1896, now a subaltern (a commissioned officer below the rank of captain) in the Fourth Hussars, Churchill sailed for India on the SS *Britannia*. In Bangalore he got his first real taste of polo, a sport valuable for the cavalry skills it taught, but that was being phased out at Sandhurst because of its prohibitive expense.

Churchill never considered polo just a game. Without exaggeration he saw it as a purpose of life. In *The Age of Churchill*, Peter de Mendelssohn wrote that young Winston "was among the best players in his regiment. The game fascinated him all his life. He never showed much liking for golf, and played it desultorily. But polo he played for the last time in Malta, in 1926, when he was 52."

At first India was a lonely place for him. "Nice people in India are few and far between. . . . [I am] poked away in a garrison town which resembles a 3rd rate watering place out of season and without the sea. . . . My life here would be intolerable were it not for the consolations of literature. . . . The only valuable knowledge I take away from India (soldiering apart) could have been gathered equally well in Cumberland Place."

Bangalore had its compensations. The town stood a cool three thousand feet above sea level. Churchill lived in a large bungalow with a staff that included a butler, houseboy, and groom. (Cheap help was a major reason that so many Englishmen endured extreme climates.) His garden grew seventy different varieties of roses. He personally taxidermed sixty-five species of butterflies. One afternoon he played in a polo match at Hyderabad that featured a parade of elephants dragging cannons and saluting with their trunks. (An elephant's trunk contains one hundred thousand muscles.)

"Mr. Churchill was a real live one," recalled his top sergeant. "The great thing about him was the way he worked. He was busier than half the others put together. I never saw him without pencils sticking out all over him. And once when I went into his bungalow I could scarcely get in what with all the books and papers and foolscap all over the place."

Churchill was a good polo player and excellent at his position: the lightweight galloping ahead of the pack. Wrote Aga Khan III (1877–1957): "It was at Poona in the late summer [in fact, early autumn] of 1896 that our paths first crossed. A group of officers of the Fourth Hussars, then stationed at Bangalore, called on me. I was ill at the time, but my cousin showed them my horses. He later told me that among them none had a keener, more discriminating eye, none was a better judge of a horse, than a young subaltern by the name of Winston Spencer Churchill."

Two months after his arrival in India, Churchill wrote to his mother: ". . . the entire population turns out to watch [a polo game] and betting not infrequently runs into thousands of rupees. Our final match against the Native contingent was witnessed by 8 or 9 thousand natives who wildly cheered every goal or stroke made by their countrymen. . . ."

From his earliest days in India, Churchill was prone to injuries, polo and otherwise, serious and not so. In this respect he was like Hemingway. Both men took unnecessary chances and were often careless and made others around them careless. A fearful hidden inadequacy was coupled with a powerful and dangerous sense of ordainment.

One day Winston accidentally attached his horse's reins to the bridle instead of the bit and rode off in all directions. Then he banged up his knee in a fall and couldn't play polo for two weeks. "Such a nuisance! I write this letter recumbent in a long chair on my verandah."

He was put in charge of regimental target practice. A bullet splintered the iron edge of a target, and flying shrapnel damaged his thumb. He in-

Winston Churchill, far past his prime,
followed closely by the Prince of Wales,
later Edward VIII, c. 1924

vited sympathy from his parents: "I am now indeed a cripple," he wrote home. "My left hand is closely bound up and useless. My right arm is so stiff I cannot brush my hair and only with difficulty my teeth." He might have been describing in typically dramatic fashion wounds suffered in combat. "However, I am healing beautifully and yesterday I managed to play polo with the reins fastened on my wrist."

Three years later, having decided that military life was a dead end, he returned to India as a roving correspondent (though still technically in the army), determined to win the Inter-Regimental Tournament, India's most prestigious sporting event.

In February 1899 he wrote to his younger brother Jack: "I am staying [in Jodhpur] with Sir Pertab Singh for a week before the Inter-Regimental tournament. All the rest of our team are here and everything smiled until last night—when I fell downstairs and sprained both my ankles and dislocated my right shoulder. . . ."

Perhaps this incident marked the beginning of a lifelong fondness for the companionship of brandy.

"I fear I shall not be able to play in the tournament. . . . It is one of the most unfortunate things that I have ever had happen to me and is a bitter disappointment. I have been playing well and my loss is a considerable blow to our chances of winning. I try to be philosophic but it is very hard. Of course it is better to have bad luck in the minor pleasures of life than in one's bigger undertakings. But I am very low and unhappy about it."

His three teammates on the Fourth Hussars decided that a crippled Churchill was better than no Churchill at all. He played through the tournament with his right shoulder strapped up, severely restricting the arc of his swing. Even so, he scored several times on dainty tap-ins at the goalmouth and was able to write to his mother on March 3, 1899: "You will be glad to hear that we won the Inter-Regimental Polo Tournament—a very great triumph for it is perhaps the biggest sporting event in India. I hit three goals out of four in the winning match so that my journey to India was not futile as far as the regiment was concerned."

Churchill did not exaggerate the thrill of victory. In one match his task was to guard Major Hardress Lloyd, a brilliant player of that era. In the 1920s, Lloyd would captain England against the United States in international matches.

Obviously Major Lloyd knew his way around a polo field. Winston's effectively neutralizing him despite his disability was a tribute to his skill. "My shoulder and arms are still vy [*sic*] weak," he wrote his mother, "and I have to play all tied up which weakens us a good deal."

For his next adventure he sailed off to South Africa in October 1899 to cover the Boer War. He got captured by and immediately escaped from the enemy. The Boers put up wanted posters all over Pretoria: "Englishman 25 years old, about 5 ft. 8 in. tall, average build, walks with a slight stoop, pale appearance, red brown hair . . . cannot pronounce the letter 'S.' "

Subsequently, Churchill's exciting book and lectures about the Boer experience made him a celebrity in England, propelling him into political history for the first time.

THE COLLAPSE of the British Empire meant an end to the games of empire. Royal Indian states, maharajas, great houses, the platoons of servants, faded away. There was no one left to play polo with.

When Dickie Mountbatten came out to India in the 1920s, on his very first day in the country, he played in the first polo game of his life in the morning. That afternoon he went on a pig-sticking hunt, spearing a wild boar from a speeding Rolls-Royce.

By the early 1920s the world's most sumptuous lifestyle was coming to an end. All the maharajas wanted to be English. "On the warmest days, they dressed for London ..."

Prep schools were formed, modeled on Eton but with slight differences. Students arrived at class aboard their elephants, accompanied by their child brides.

The Indian rulers adopted coats of arms, Latin mottoes; they grappled for knighthoods, were delighted when the king of England awarded them the Star of India or the Order of the Indian Empire. The big social events were held not in Indian palaces but at the British viceregal palace in Calcutta or New Delhi.

Declared a British viceroy to an assemblage of Indian royalty (and one can imagine the tone): "The Emperor of China and I rule half the world and still have time for breakfast."

The Indian rulers were reduced to luxurious vassalage. They installed dressing rooms to hold their "newly acquired Western clothes. The largest belonged to the sixth Nizam of Hyderabad, Mahbub Ali Khan. It filled an entire wing of his palace and stood two stories high. Made of Burma teak, it resembled a cloister more than a cupboard. Two hand-managed lifts brought down life-sized dummies in garments the Nizam might be tempted to wear—although the fastidious Mahbub Ali Khan is reported never to have worn a garment twice."

Indian rulers became exotic entertainers to European nobility. The kingdom of Birkaner was famous for its sandgrouse "shoot." In one day, fourteen shotguns accounted for eleven thousand birds. A wag observed that the king of Birkaner ruled by "the grouse of God."

The British had their unique way of letting a maharaja know whether he was coming or going. They had the simple expedient of the gun salute. A maharaja got a twenty-one-gun salute from the British if he'd been good, but sank to as low as fifteen guns if he had displeased.

V. S. Naipaul put it best in another context about another social class. "To awaken to history was to cease to live instinctively. It was to begin to see oneself and one's group the way the outside world saw one; and it was to know a kind of rage."

From exile, the last of the Moghul emperors wrote:

> *All that I loved is gone*
> *Like a garden robbed of its beauty by autumn,*
> *I am only a memory of splendour.*

There was no need for poetry in the cosmopolitan world opened up to Indian royalty by the British Raj. A fragment of a 1920s pop song will do, hardly more than a limerick but once the rage of Europe:

> *There was a rich Maharaja of Magador*
> *Who had ten thousand camels and maybe more*
> *He had rubies and pearls and the loveliest girls*
> *But he didn't know how to do the rhumba. . . .*

The refrain:

> *Rhumba lessons are wanted for*
> *The rich Maharaja of Magador.*

FROM HIS EARLIEST DAYS Dickie Mountbatten was infatuated with polo. Though not a good player himself, he performed an invaluable service to the game by codifying its disparate rules.

In the early 1930s, under the aegis of the Royal Naval Polo Association, and using the pseudonym "Marco," Mountbatten wrote *An Intro-duction to Polo.*

The book has remained a classic of its kind, setting forth clearly the duties of a polo player, offering instruction on team play and striking the ball. There is advice on almost everything except horsemanship. It was assumed that a gentleman knew how to ride.

The rules have changed little in sixty years. Two teams of four horse-men play on a rectangular grass field 12.4 acres in size, 300 yards long and 200 wide if unboarded, 300 yards long and 160 wide if boarded.

Each team is divided into four positions—1, 2, 3, and 4. Number 4 is also called the back. Numbers 1, 2, and 3 are with variations considered offensive positions, though in a fast-moving game distinctions are often blurred. For example, the back may decide to play offense in a particular situation, while number 3 will drop back to defense.

Number 1's job is to guard the opposition's back, and number 2's is to guard his opposite at number 3. Again, in the best polo everything is fluid and subject to change within the space of a hoofbeat.

Generally, a game is divided into six or eight periods of seven and a half minutes each. The average match lasts about ninety minutes, with an intermission during which the fans may go out onto the field to re-place divots or walk over to admire the horses.

The players use croquetlike mallets 50 to 53 inches in length. The polo ball is made of willow root or compressed plastic, $3^1/_4$ inches in di-ameter, weighing about $4^1/_2$ ounces. Fixed but collapsible goalposts stand 24 feet apart at opposite ends of the field.

The most important rule in polo is that of right-of-way. If a player has the ball on his mallet, or is heading in a straight line toward a ball that he has just hit, he may not be interfered with, nor may his line toward the ball be crossed. This rule is sternly enforced to help avoid accidents.

Baseball fans have seen collisions in the outfield between players vying for a ball. These are nothing compared with what happens when a horse going thirty-five miles per hour runs into another horse that is either standing still or traveling at the same speed. Death may result, and has—to horse, rider, and both.

Polo horses are the smartest of all trained animals. It is a ghastly sight when one is killed on the grass. I am always reminded of poet Robinson Jeffers's line about another magnificent creature: "Excepting the penalties, I'd sooner kill a man than a hawk."

Polo players are ranked, or handicapped, from minus-two goals at the lowest to ten goals at the highest. Forty-three players have reached a handicap of ten goals since 1890, twenty-three of them from North America. Only 175 players in history have ever been ranked at seven goals or above. The gap between the skills of the top and bottom ranks in polo is perhaps the widest of any sport.

POLO IS EASY to play but significantly hard to play well. In my opinion the game has produced four immortals. Cast in positional order as my own dream team, they are:

1. Leslie St. Clair Cheape (England), 1882–1916
2. Thomas Hitchcock, Jr. (United States), 1900–1944
3. Juan Carlos Harriott (Argentina), 1936–present
4. John Watson (Ireland), 1820–1898

Leslie Cheape dominated international polo in its brief golden age, the years 1913 and 1914.

Tommy Hitchcock was polo's Babe Ruth.

Juan Carlos Harriott was the greatest player of the post–World War II era.

Above: Tommy Hitchcock, 1927
Left: Juan Carlos Harriott, c. 1979

John Watson invented the backhand shot, brought system to the sport in its early years, and was the best player of the nineteenth century.

In addition to the rules and regulations, it must be remembered that polo was not always an elitist excitement for the rich. Once upon a time the sport had mass appeal. In the 1920s, forty thousand fans often showed up for a game. Special trains were laid on by the Long Island Rail Road to transport people out to the Meadow Brook Club in Westbury for an international match between England and the United States.

In 1924, 120,000 fans in New Delhi, India, watched a polo match. So many fans were eager to see the game that riots nearly resulted.

American stable yard at Hurlingham, 1921

Chapter Two

I T BEGAN IN TIBET—probably—two thousand years and more ago and was called *pulu*, Tibetan for "willow root." The game spread to the royal courts of Persia, with twenty or so riders to a side using sticks that resembled primitive golf clubs. The technique was to dribble, not pass, the ball upfield. Polo sticks were so fragile that each player had a bearer who carried bouquets of extras.

In a small town in north-central Iran stand centuries-old goalposts made of bullet-shaped stones about three feet high. The Persian game involved more milling around than action, which was to be expected when forty players trotted up and down a field considerably smaller than that used in modern polo.

The goalposts are located in the town square, indicating that these *chaugan* games—as polo was called in Persia—were a central attraction, mainly because of their danger. Accidentally falling on a goalpost was a good way for a player to get eviscerated, like being splayed on an enormous juicer.

Persian poetry and literature are saturated with polo imagery, but it is difficult to separate fact from romance. A man named Gushtasp was such a tremendous hitter "that the ball could no longer be seen by any person on the meidan, or plain, as his blow had caused it to vanish among the clouds."

Alexander the Great had a polo moment. In 333 B.C., he refused to pay a tribute to Darius, the Persian king. Darius sent Alexander a polo stick and ball to indicate that the brash upstart would be better off playing polo than engaging in warlike pursuits.

Alexander didn't get to be the greatest by being modest: he replied to Darius that the ball was the earth, and he—Alexander—was the stick.

One young Persian member of court was described exaltedly around A.D. 1530: "He was a man of courage, an excellent archer, and remarkable for his skill in playing the games of chaugan and leap-frog." Of course, leapfrog died out with the invention of the Prussian spiked helmet.

After Tamerlane conquered most of what is now the Middle East, polo and good manners took a turn for the worse. A favorite imprecation became "May we play with your heads as if they were chaugan balls."

It was widely believed in legend that Tamerlane played polo with the heads of his slain enemies. If so, the game was on the slow side, since a human head weighs twelve pounds.

English explorers and traders have left several vivid accounts of Persian polo. Here is an English traveler's description of a game in 1599:

After the banquet was ended the King requested Sir Anthony [Sherley] to look through the window to behold their sports on horseback. Before the house there was a very fair place, to the quantity of some ten acres of ground, made very plain; so the King went down, and when he had taken his horse the drums and trumpets sounded.

There were twelve horsemen in all with the King; so they divided themselves, six on the one side and six on the other, having in their hands long rods of wood about the bigness of a man's finger, and at one end of the rods a piece of wood nailed like a hammer.

After they were divided and turned face to face, there came one in the middle, and threw a ball between both the companies, and having goals made at either end of the plain, they began their sport, striking the ball with their rods from one to the other, in the fashion of our football play here in England; and ever when the King had gotten the ball before him the drums and trumpets would play one alarum, and many times the King would come to Sir Anthony at the window and ask him how he did like the sport.

And this sublime account from a sixteenth-century court historian:

His Majesty also plays chaugan on dark nights, which caused much astonishment, even among clever players. The balls which are used at night are set on fire. For this purpose palas [balsa?] wood is used, which is very light and burns for a long time. For the sake of adding splendor to the games, which is necessary in worldly matters, his Majesty has knobs of gold and silver fixed to the top of the chaugan sticks. If one of them breaks, any player that gets hold of the pieces may keep them.

It is impossible to describe the excellence of this game. Ignorant as I am, I can say but little about it.

In Persian literature polo is often used heavily as metaphor. A personal favorite helps the modern spirit abide: "Man is a ball tossed into the field of existence, driven hither and thither by the chaugan-stick of destiny, wielded by the hand of Providence."

And, to set a romantic mood: "The heart of a lover is the ball, while the curling love-lock of his charmer is as the curved club that impels it."

FROM PERSIA AND TIBET the game spread to northern India. There it ran up against an imperial British style that regarded polo as fit only for "noble savages."

British observers condescended to watch the lively proceedings among the natives. Here is one account from the Badminton Library:

> Whilst the game progressed the combined bands played a selection of music which depended for its piano, crescendo, forte, and fortissimo effects on the character of the play, a good run being greeted with a banging of tom-toms and loud trumpetings, whilst a sudden drop to pianissimo condemned a bit of slow play or a total miss. To give the players their due most of the music was of a very vigorous character.
>
> The gallop and hit-off, especially if the latter was successful, were the occasions of redoubled efforts; but the moments for which the musicians really longed were when the Rajah galloped with the ball; then two enormous horns, about twelve feet long, with bells at the end which could have covered a small boy like an extinguisher, were reared slowly up to a horizontal position, the tom-tom wallahs grasped their sticks, and the Zillah Sahib's chief trumpeter distended himself with air, and, as their ruler started on his ride, every musician chose the note which experience told him was the most powerful that his instrument had, and blew his immortal soul into it. . . .
>
> So the game progressed, amid much excitement, till there came a truly civilized pause for refreshment, which appealed to my sympathies in a most natural manner. They did not run to whisky and soda, however, and, instead of cigarettes, passed round a large bubble-bubble [water pipe]. Then there was more galloping, more hitting-off of the ball, with the usual accompaniment of horrid sounds and harder riding than ever, varied by one stout gentleman in voluminous white garments, whose pony pecked and deposited him with a terrible souse on the broad of his back; yards of puggree [a long scarf wrapped round the helmet and falling over the neck] flew about the ground, with considerable disarrangement of his remaining attire, but he was immediately surrounded by sympathizing menials, who gradually swathed him into shape again, the ball meantime flying about the ground, with riders dashing after it, as if this interesting toilet were going on a hundred miles off, instead of in their midst.

The game caught on particularly well in the independent Indian state of Manipur, where, nestled between the provinces of Assam and Cachar, the British took hold of it.

It is fair to say that polo as we know it began in Manipur, in a green valley amid high mountains, where beyond rose the Himalayas.

The Manipurees played on tiny ponies, overweighted with saddles of up to thirty pounds. The ponies, strong and wiry, easily bore saddle and man. "The Manipurees invariably carry a whip made of plaited thongs of raw hide slung on the left wrist, though where they managed to hit their ponies, covered as they are with leather and trappings, is a mystery."

Wrote a Major General Scherer to a British sporting magazine: ". . . the Manipurees, with their long, streaming hair, their bodies naked to the waist, their quaint saddlery, and excited demeanour, give one a fair idea of the noble savage thoroughly enjoying himself."

The confident General Scherer got up a British team to challenge the Manipurees. The "savages" handed him his lunch. "The Manipurees, again, were no respecters of persons," wrote the shocked general. "It was quite permissible, and recognized as lawful, to ride at and through anything or anybody that came between the player and the spot where the ball lay. I was once caught in this position and dilemma, and was simply sent spinning, pony and all, and got considerably shaken and bruised."

The game spread throughout India to all the British regiments. Rules were codified, and four men to a side became mandatory. "Seven or eight ponies apiece are now not uncommon, and if a man does not 'play the game,' he is hopelessly 'out of it.'"

In 1876 in New Delhi, representatives of most British regiments in the empire met and decided to hold the annual Inter-Regimental Tournament. "Right pleasant too are these great gatherings, when men from all parts of the empire congregate, and there is no surer place of meeting for old and widely scattered 'pals' than the Indian polo tournaments."

Englishwomen took up the sport to a degree, and one match in particular, described in an 1873 book called *Polo in India*, by Captain G. F. Younghusband, is worth quoting in full for its Victorian flavor:

> The match was between four married ladies and four single ones, each side being allowed one of the opposite and more brutal sex to act as a support and backbone to the team; but it was specially ordained that neither of them was to go up into the game and hit the ball about too much, or hustle in an unladylike manner.
>
> The game was a very fast and good one for about a minute, and then one of the unmarried ladies called a halt, on the ground that her veil was dreadfully in the way, and she must really take it off—which she accordingly did, whilst everyone waited—and the male member of the team was called up and ordered to put it in his pocket; an unreasonable and even tyrannical request when made to a man with next to no clothing on, and certainly no pockets in it.
>
> Another minute of stern and businesslike play—during which the two teams managed to hit the ball three distinct times between them—and then Mrs. A declared she could play no longer with gloves on, because she could not hold her stick properly; and Mrs. B, having played so far without gloves, taking the opposite view, said she could play no longer without gloves, and that her rings hurt her dreadfully. So these two went off to the touch line, the one to take off her gloves, and the other to put them on.
>
> This was a famous opportunity for all the rest of the party to discover that something or other was wrong with them, their ponies or their get-up.
>
> Having soothed and set straight everybody, the two males get off their ponies, light cigars, and sit down on the ground to await the development of affairs. After a quarter of an hour's rest, they developed into another three minutes' play, during which a considerable improvement in the all-round play was noticeable, and one of the males hit a

goal for his side, much to the indignation of all the ladies on the other side.

Then followed two minutes' more play, during which the other male, incited thereto by the reproofs liberally administered to him by his own side, hit a corresponding goal for them.

By the nature of things it was now, in the ordinary course of events, tea-time, and an adjournment for this necessary meal was at once decided upon. After tea, which occupied one way or another about half an hour, play was resumed. Every one seemed greatly revived, and some really good runs were made.

It is quite exciting what wonders tea works on the female constitution. So in our game tea made all the difference, and the play afterwards was really astonishingly good, considering the inexperience of the players. Having the offside [the rider's right side] of the pony quite clear [presumably because the women rode sidesaddle], they could get a clean hit on that side, and those on handy, well-trained ponies appeared to be very nearly as active after the ball as men would be.

As long as ladies play only in a ladies' game, and ride handy, well-trained ponies, there is no reason why polo should not, like hunting, become a pastime for our sisters and cousins and aunts as well as for ourselves. To return to our match. After, in all, about twenty minutes' play, it was voted that the game should be declared drawn, everyone being too hot and tired to go on.

According to Newell Bent in his excellent book *American Polo* (New York, 1929), polo was also played in Japan and China a thousand years ago. The Japanese game still survives to the modern day as *dai-kiu*, or "ball match." Oddly enough, the goalposts in ancient history were placed twenty-four feet apart, as they are today. The object of the Japanese and Chinese game, however, was to hit a paper ball covered with bamboo fiber into a hole one foot in diameter. The Chinese used only one goal and frequently rode donkeys instead of horses.

After polo became the rage in India, it was only a matter of time before the game made its way to England. The precise moment of conception is recorded in the Badminton Library's *History of Polo* (1891). Its account has never been seriously challenged.

> It is generally supposed that the origin of the game in England was due to a cavalry regiment lately returned from India; that they had seen the game there, and so brought the idea with them. This theory is, however, erroneous. It originated in a far more prosaic manner, and found its birthplace in the brain of sundry young subalterns of the 10th Hussars in 1869. This regiment was then quartered in Aldershot under canvas. After lunch one day, and wearying for some occupation wherewith to kill time and overcome the ennui of camp life, Messrs. St. Quintin, 'Chicken' Hartopp, and Chain were scanning the papers in the ante-room tent. There they read an account of the game as played by the Manipurees. Quoth one [believed to be Chicken Hartopp]: "By Jove! it must be a goodish game. I vote we try it."
>
> No sooner said than done. Their chargers were saddled, crooked sticks and a billiard ball got hold of, and they set to work—needless to say with no great results.... At this early period of the game it was called "hockey on horseback." Soon regiments of Hussars and Lancers were challenging each other on British soil, and the great game began.

I can find nothing more in history about Chicken Hartopp, except a note that he was extremely obese.

Polo didn't take off in England until 1873. The prestigious Hurlingham Club sponsored the sport as "an attraction in addition to the pigeon shooting." The game thus became separated from its regimental origins and was played by civilians for the first time.

The finest player of the nineteenth century was the burly Irishman John Watson. In 1886 he led an excellent Hurlingham team against a foursome of Americans on a small but well-kept field at Newport, Rhode Island. The Americans, at this time tyros at polo, lost badly. The British credited their opponents with working hard and hitting well, but noted that the Americans were at a disadvantage because they rode mustang ponies of considerable dexterity but no speed.

The father of American polo—as opposed to Harry Payne Whitney, who was the father of modern polo—was the newspaper magnate James Gordon Bennett. Bennett was in the mold of William Randolph Hearst and Joseph Pulitzer: a you-get-the-pictures-I'll-make-the-war press baron of the kind much beloved by star journalists like Stephen Crane and Richard Harding Davis, who commanded exorbitant sums for covering wars from the Crimea to Cuba.

In 1869, as editor-in-chief of the New York *Herald*, Bennett sent Henry Morton Stanley to locate Dr. Livingstone, who was living in the village of Ujiji on Lake Tanganyika in Africa.

Described by contemporaries as petty and tyrannical with his subordinates in the newspaper business, Bennett earned this accolade from Newell Bent: "one of the best and most liberal patrons of sport our country has ever known."

On a visit to England in 1876 Bennett saw his first polo game at the Hurlingham Club. He was impressed by the action and particularly the physical fitness of British cavalrymen. The Little Bighorn massacre had occurred earlier that year in Montana, and Bennett might have decided that toughening up was needed to prevent more tragedies. Polo was perfect cavalry training. It also didn't hurt in Bennett's eyes that polo was so visibly a rich man's sport. The sheer expense would keep the riffraff at baseball games.

Before leaving England, Bennett collected some sticks and balls and once back in New York sent a riding master named Harry Blasson to Texas to buy mustangs.

The first polo game ever held in the United States was played indoors in the winter of 1876 in New York City at a place called Dickel's Riding

Academy, located at the corner of Fifth Avenue and Thirty-ninth Street in Manhattan. Dickel's was later torn down and replaced by the Union League Club.

The Westchester Polo Club was formed by Bennett and other swells, and the club eventually found a permanent home at the Polo Grounds on 156th Street, which years later became the playground of Willie Mays.

In 1878 Bennett retired from the game to pursue his other interests, including financing Stanley's Congo expedition. He sold the best of his Texas ponies for eighty-five dollars.

In quick succession the Meadow Brook Club—America's Hurlingham—was formed, followed by the Brighton Polo Club in Long Branch, New Jersey. At Brighton there was a dearth of mallets and balls, so croquet sets were used. The croquet mallet head was fastened onto a hay-rake handle, and croquet balls served as polo balls.

Presiding at the creation of the Brighton Polo Club was a genial, heavyset man named H. L. Herbert. In 1890 he became the first chairman of the U.S. Polo Association.

The Brighton members started from scratch. There must have been wild scenes of runaway horses before a decent game took place. "It happened that a number of ponies from a Texas ranch had arrived at Long Branch to be sold," wrote Herbert. "Some of them were broken to saddle, but none had ever seen a polo [or croquet] mallet, nor had the half-dozen men who were sitting on the porch of a near-by seaside cottage any more knowledge of the game than the newspaper account of 'shinny [field hockey] on horseback' had given them."

On June 21, 1879, ten thousand fans saw a polo game at the Military Parade Ground in Prospect Park, Brooklyn. The match was played between Westchester and the Queens County Club, founded by August Belmont. On this day Belmont played for Westchester, and Herbert

Three spectators, Aiken, South Carolina,
1933

recorded the disorganized scene: "Team play was then unknown and the hero of the day was the individual who could score the greatest number of goals regardless of the others on his side. The play consisted mostly of a huddling, pushing, shouting mass, and few had the skill to race very far with the ball."

Herbert noted the primitive level at which polo was then played: "Almost the first attempt at team play was an arrangement between Mr. Belmont and myself, who were on the Westchester team, by which I was to ride into the scrimmage and pass the ball out to Mr. Belmont, who would rush away with it to the goal, with the result that the Queens County Club was whitewashed."

Clubs sprang up in Boston, Buffalo, and Philadelphia. In 1890 the Oyster Bay Polo Club on Long Island was formed by Theodore and Elliott Roosevelt, among others. Recalled T.R.'s wife, Edith: "We were all young and gay in 1890 and found much amusement in polo of the most amateur variety."

No photograph exists of Theodore Roosevelt playing polo, but he did achieve a handicap of one goal and played for his club. A silver tobacco jar sits in his library at Sagamore Hill, inscribed:

POLO

July 5, 1890
Blues vs. Reds

WINNERS:

1. E. Willard Robey   3. Walter Tuckerman
2. Theodore Roosevelt 4. B. Munro Ferguson

Wrote the great man himself on July 15, 1890: "I tell you a corpulent middle-aged literary man finds a stiff polo match rather good exercise."

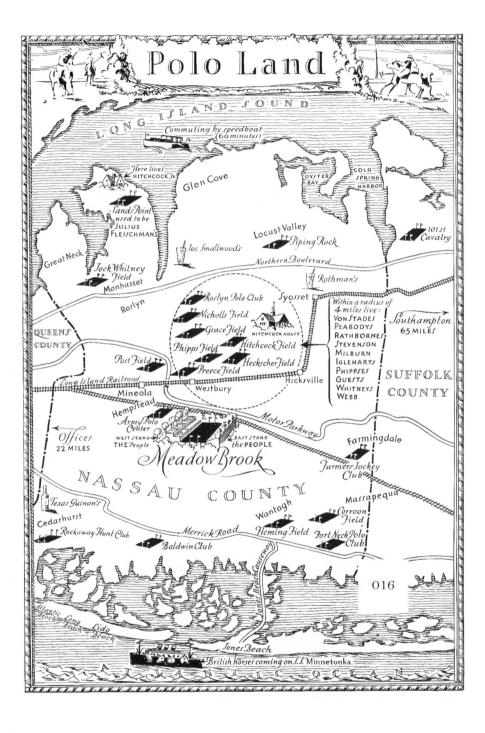

Polo Land

LONG ISLAND SOUND

Commuting by speedboat
(60 minutes)

Here lives
HITCHCOCK, Jr.

Glen Cove

OYSTER BAY

COLD SPRING HARBOR

Sands Point
used to be
JULIUS FLEISCHMANS

Locust Valley

Piping Rock

101st Cavalry

Joe Smallwood's

Northern Boulevard

Great Neck

Jock Whitney Field
Manhasset

Rothman's

Rorlyn

Roslyn Polo Club

Syosset

Within a radius of
4 miles live:
VON STADES
PEABODYS
RATHBORNES
STEVENSON
MILBURN
IGLEHARTS
PHIPPSES
GUESTS
WHITNEYS
WEBB

Southampton
65 MILES

Nicholls Field

Grace Field

HITCHCOCK HOUSE

QUEENS COUNTY

Phipps Field

Hitchcock Field

Post Field

Heckscher Field

SUFFOLK COUNTY

Long Island Railroad

Preece Field

Westbury

Hicksville

Mineola

Hempstead

Army Polo Center

Motor Parkway

Farmingdale

Offices
22 MILES

WEST STAND
THE PEOPLE

EAST STAND
the PEOPLE

Meadow Brook

Farmers Jockey Club

NASSAU   COUNTY

Massapequa

Texas Guinan's

Corroon Field

Cedarhurst

Wantagh

Rockaway Hunt Club

Merrick Road

Fleming Field

Fort Neck Polo Club

Baldwin Club

016

Atlantic Beach
Long Beach
Lido Beach

Jones Beach

British horses coming on S.S. Minnetonka

ATLANTIC   OCEAN

Chapter Three

FOR A LONG TIME I used to get up an hour before dawn. I remember the winters in particular, when I would go horseback riding through the last sections of fields and woods on the North Shore of Long Island. That countryside once was the world center of polo.

The horse gathered itself under me, lowered its haunches, raised its head, and stutter-stepped in preparation for the gallop, snorting winter wind, mouth flecked with white. . . .

One field in particular, fringed with dense woods, was as large as thirty polo fields. I crouched into a semi–jockey position, close to the horse's mane. The big hunter wore itself out after a lap or two around the field, slowed down to a canter, and finally a walk. The day seemed breathlessly gifted with possibilities, with so much daylight until dark.

Horses ran in my family, so to speak.

The field exists no longer, nor the woods. Families have dispersed and sold their estates. Developments stand where once the rich had their private golf courses, riding rings, indoor tennis courts, and pools.

Most of the land has been parceled into smaller plots. New houses have been built in a Georgian or Mediterranean style and sell for millions of dollars apiece. These developments have names like Bridle Path Estates and the Hamlet.

Old Westbury and Westbury had originally been Quaker farming communities before the turn-of-the-century discovery of their unbroken landscapes. The villages were just twenty-five miles east of New York City, with room enough for polo fields, hunting trails, and running fences.

It had to be, eventually, as generations passed away, that a developer would look at acres of unused polo fields and buy the land for office buildings or condominiums. The land was especially valuable because it was located so close to the Long Island Expressway.

The scenic field of so many of my winter gallops is now the campus of the State University of New York at Old Westbury, with its large, white modernistic buildings and asphalt drives. Sometimes I go over there to jog, but the field no longer has compass points for me.

The expressway was built in 1955 and did in the countryside. By then most of the men and women of power and money were decrepit or dead or living in Palm Beach or Hobe Sound. No one was powerful enough to stop Robert Moses, the state highway commissioner, from sticking his new road anywhere he wanted. One of the places he most wanted to stick it was through Old Westbury.

Moses had his reasons. He had been bested once by the village's residents during the building of the Northern State Parkway in the 1930s. Motorists have noticed while driving along this lovely road—perhaps toward summerhouses or beaches in the Hamptons—that it makes a five-mile detour at Old Westbury. The Old Guard wanted nothing to disturb their pristine environment.

The Long Island Expressway is renowned today as the world's longest parking lot.

Mostly, I remember the horses, the huge hunters, all in memory the color of winter sky. With skilled riders aboard, they led the pack at every hunt, cleared post-and-rail fences with inches to spare.

Springs and summers were for polo horses. They had these gaits, wonderful rocking-chair canters and arrow-straight gallops. I never got used to their extraordinary reflexes. They shifted gears and stopped and started so quickly that one minute I was comfortably in the saddle, the next flat on the grass. They waited patiently for me to reboard. They were just the right size not to be intimidating, and I never had the sense of having a long way to fall.

People talk about the acceleration of a car, but a polo horse will take a rider from zero to thirty-five miles per hour in three seconds. There were moments of concert, cowboy joy, length-of-the-field races that might have bounded on forever in the hot afternoon, not dawn this time. I had a glimmer of, well, togetherness, and some distant, hitherto unthinkable joy.

I went away to prep school and took up sports firmly grounded on the ground. Baseball, football, and ice hockey meant an end to riding.

My childhood formed a triad: first, the hunter dawn; second, the polo-pony afternoon; third, the game itself.

My father, Devereux Milburn, Jr., played as often as three times a week in summer, usually practice games Tuesday and Thursday in the early evenings—when he took the train out from his law firm in New York—and then the big game on Saturday or Sunday at the Meadow Brook Club or Bostwick Field. Once a year he went to Oak Brook, outside of Chicago, to play in the United States Open. He retired from polo in 1957, after bone chips were removed from his elbow.

My father played the defensive, or back, position. He was a good player and a thoughtful one. He rarely hit the ball without an idea of

*Two future poloists jumping fences
on Long Island*

where he wanted it to go. This can be taught in practice, but having an idea—or "having an idea out there," a baseball expression I've borrowed for polo—is not easy with opposing players breathing down your neck. He seldom missed. One of the ideas of polo is not to miss.

My father did not have a hard shot or the feral energy great players often possess. When I saw Prince Charles play in England, I was reminded of my father's style. Both players protected their own goal at all costs and played cerebral mistake-free polo that made them assets to any team.

Playing defense well requires forethought and execution—two qualities that are difficult to learn but give polo its occasional subtlety. As in high-speed chess, a back must rely on the instincts of intelligence. He must know where everyone is on the field at all times and be able to forecast plays: If this happens, I will do this; if that happens, I will be over there.

Ironically, the novice is usually put on defense, so he can be kept far from the action and not do any damage. Defense is easy to play if the idea is merely to show up, but hard to play well. I can name twenty great number 1's or 2's or 3's, but not more than five great number 4's.

Most players want to participate in the glamour of attack, make the field-halving shot no matter where it goes. The intricate quality of play involved in defense is not glamorous. A deft save often goes unnoticed, but a whiff forgiven at midfield is never forgiven in the mouth of one's own goal.

UNTIL I WAS twelve years old, I went to polo matches as often as another kid might go to baseball games—if his father was a professional baseball player. I never considered that it took lots of money to buy horses, hire grooms, maintain fields—all of that. I was too far inside the game and too young to make those economic connections.

The game was violent. The closer to the field I got, the more violent it became. Polo is a contact sport and sometimes a collision sport. This fact often leads to grudges, paybacks, and a general harshness of tone. Otherwise gentlemanly people lose their cool on a polo field.

I hated that aspect of it—the yelling. I identified strongly with the main character in the children's book *Ferdinand the Bull*, who wanted to sit in a field all day and smell the flowers.

I usually watched polo games from the sidelines near the steaming horses and bustling grooms. I witnessed intra- and interteam arguments that could turn bitter. Some players whined; some got into debates with referees; others were strutting egoists; some were all three, besides shouting at their grooms, which even as a child I thought was unforgivable.

For many people polo represents the height of effeteness. That wasn't the way I saw it. I observed horses upended and flailing hooves. I always felt as if I were standing in the middle of a cavalry charge, and at the last second the horses parted for me.

Occasionally, my father played a big match before a good crowd, affording me an opportunity to sit in the grandstand at a safe distance from the field. I remember one game in which the prizes stood on a large table near the sideboards. There was a large silver trophy, silver cigarette boxes, and a row of plaid ice chests, each one about two feet high.

Sitting up there in the grandstand with my mother and two older brothers, I surveyed the field from heights of remote grandeur. Players seemed very far away, their actions muted. I didn't have to concentrate on the game at all. I paid attention to the brightness of green field, glinting trophies, players' colorful uniforms, unthreatening horses, powder-blue goalposts, all of it miniaturized to a size that I was finally able to deal with.

A peculiar happiness swept over me at this pageant. I wanted to stretch the moment, to make that Eskimo Pie or toasted-almond Good Humor bar a columned entrance to the enchantments of childhood.

My father seized the pretty interval to make a rare offensive foray along the sideboards nearest the grandstand. He rode a speedy horse, he had the ball, and his charge was spectacular—all that muffled thunder of gallop. I didn't like races along the sideboards. It was a good way to get killed if a horse stumbled against the unyielding wood.

He made this long run, and the crowd of perhaps five thousand—excellent for a sport in its postwar death throes—hushed, because here was a thrill in a game that keeps its distance.

My father shouted into the green stillness, "Get out of my way, you son of a bitch!" I didn't know if he yelled at teammate or opponent, but he was going all the way with this one. I couldn't understand what had gotten into him, since he really didn't like this high-speed stuff.

I wished that his "son of a bitch" hadn't hung for so long over the grandstand. Having the standard capacity of a child to experience utter mortification, I would have much preferred my father to exclaim jovially, "Coming through, old chap!"

He had this whole avenue to himself, bordered by the sideboard on one side, a rim of milling players on the other.

He hit a bullet, low and rising. The shot flew wildly off-line. With a resounding crunch, the ball struck a plaid ice chest on the sidelines, which tottered from the blow. The ball dropped away, out-of-bounds.

At the presentation ceremonies after the game, to much laughter, my father was presented with the dented ice chest, which he accepted graciously. For a long time it stood in the bar of our house on Long Island.

THE PLACE of my hunter dawns was named Clark's Field after Ambrose Clark, an industrial magnate and sportsman. He was often to be seen, an aged man wrapped in a heavy coat with a colorful blanket draped over his knees, passing along gilded lanes in his elegant one-horse trap.

Ambrose Clark had heavyweight solidity, rock permanence, gravity. For me he was the living symbol of wealth. This or that man in the modern age would be up or down, bankrupt or indicted, full of the lightness of paper money, hustling, publicity mad. That money never counted; it floated, here today and gone tomorrow.

But Ambrose Clark, weighed down in his lovely carriage, cozy to the gills, with the lightest flicking whip and a beautiful black horse to trot before him, was a sovereign. The way he raised his arm in grave salute to passersby.

Clark would traverse one of the overpasses of the nearby expressway and turn down the creamy-chocolate tarmac of the service road. I figured that sooner or later he'd get run over, trap and all, by a dashing commuter, but he lived to a ripe age.

Ambrose Clark had the longest front driveway that I have ever seen. It stretched almost two miles under an archway of lindens and maples leading up to a redbrick Palladian mansion with a white cupola on top. The house overlooked miles of fields and stables and pastured racehorses, their tails flicking, coats glistening, as they ran away down.

The best thing about riding was meandering along the top of a hill as a dawn vista spread gold westward for thirty miles—rivers of express-

Devereux Milburn, Jr., c. 1935, at eighteen

way, sparkling cars, and far in the distance the Empire State Building, rising as though half in and half out of a sea.

The memories of my childhood are scattered, but they begin and end with riding. I saw the twilight of polo in the 1950s: the slide from the glories of the 1920s, long before its marred rebirth in the 1980s.

My parents went to England on the *Queen Mary* in 1953, where my father played in the Coronation Cup, inaugurated by Prince Philip. My brothers, sister, and I went down to the dock to see them off. Edgar Bergen, the ventriloquist, occupied an adjoining stateroom and showed us Charlie McCarthy. (I wanted to see Mortimer Snerd.) Bergen told my parents that he never put Charlie McCarthy away in his trunk when people were around.

I remember the jokes about polo. There is a wonderful sketch on "The Honeymooners" in which Ralph Kramden, aspiring to an acting career, mispronounces "polo ponies" as "puh-LAHP-uh-neez" onstage. The first time I saw the skit on television I had one of the larger laughs of my life. For days afterward I thought of those puh-LAHP-uh-neez and laughed again.

I recall several movies of the 1950s, in ripe color, in which Ricardo Montalban played a Latin American polo player in love, usually with Esther Williams. There was always a polo sequence and a swimming sequence. Red Skelton provided the comic interest in these films. He frequently wound up at the big match riding a puh-LAHP—a polo pony backward yet scoring the winning goal.

MY GRANDFATHER, Devereux Milburn, died in 1942 at the age of sixty-one. His ten-goal days were long over, but he was still ranked at seven goals and played better than his handicap. I suppose at sixty-one he was the oldest seven-goaler who ever lived.

Physically, he was a wreck. My grandmother forbade him to play polo, a rule he disregarded.

Shortly before his death, he won a nine-goal tournament—that is, the total handicap of the players on each team could not exceed nine goals—with three zero-goal players, including my father and uncle, who were then in their early twenties. My grandfather did most of the heavy lifting and spent the afternoon deflecting shots inside his own goalmouth.

He dropped dead on the Meadow Brook Club golf course in Westbury, Long Island. Family legend says he keeled over after sinking a winning putt on the eighteenth hole. Like all family legends, this one sounds embellished. I think he just dropped dead. He was overdue.

For me he remains a thoroughly fictional character left over from a premodern generation. He was a straight-ahead sort of man. It was a different age.

At sixty-one he was old; not in years, but he had subjected his body to more than one life. He was full of wires and struts and steel pins—creaking, stretching jerkily. For some portion of his older athletic career he slept with a sling device to prevent his shoulder from separating agonizingly if he moved in the night.

The combination of a steeplechase accident in Aiken, South Carolina, and a polo collision with a rough California ten-goaler with the mild-mannered name of Elmer Boeseke, Jr., effectively ended my grandfather's career at the international level. He was a ten-goal polo player until the age of forty-seven, which is ancient to be world-class.

For years I've carried around a portrait of him in full polo regalia aboard his horse. It is the first picture hung in any place that I have

Painting of Devereux Milburn, Sr.,
by Sir Alfred Munnings.

lived. The larger, original painting by Sir Alfred Munnings is in my parents' house. Occasionally the original is loaned out for polo exhibitions and then returned to its accustomed spot over the fireplace in the living room.

The print has always looked out of place in my houses and apartments. Large polo or hunting prints and English landscapes, staples of charmed Camelots in upper-class life, are gloomy, a reminder, as one historian put it, of an age when the death penalty was administered for poaching.

In the past I rarely mentioned to visitors that the portrait was of my grandfather. For a long time polo and its connotations of the high life embarrassed me, particularly during the era of Vietnam and civil rights.

A French intellectual came one night for dinner. He had a petit fit at the picture. My grandfather's portrait represented everything distasteful to him—realism, representation, horses, nineteenth-century stultification, excesses of the satin-culotted ancien régime.

The Frenchman stood in front of the portrait and turned up his nose and actually snorted. Clichés made real. He gave me a golden opportunity to neutralize polo with sociological perspective and an agreeable laugh.

(Later I came upon a fragment of the Frenchman's philosophical writings, one sentence of which began: "Heidegger and I agree . . ." He had put himself in lofty company.)

Offered this chance to deny my heritage with a fraternal smile or shrug, I didn't. He could go screw himself. True, abstractions and monochromes might easily have filled the empty spaces left by horse and rider, but I never parted with the picture. I could have offered it to one of my brothers or sisters, or abandoned it in the attic of the house in Old

Westbury among steamer trunks and blackened trophies of a bygone age. A relic with no historical life, not even memories.

My grandfather and polo died at approximately the same time, at the outset of World War II. My mother's side of the family provided us with the history we needed, gobs of Rhode Island lore, her childhood in Wickford and Narragansett and Providence, millstones grinding, and johnnycakes. My mother's history effectively masked the fact that I knew little about my father's family. The polo side.

SCRAPBOOKS sit piled in a corner of my parents' library. Covers are dusty, newspapers flaked, pictures curled. At random from the stack I pull a vivid photograph of my grandfather taking a fence in Aiken, sometime in the 1930s. While he's in the air and halfway across the fence, the jump goes terribly wrong. The photograph captures this prelude to catastrophe. The horse's forelegs have crumpled, forcing its head down. My grandfather is thrown back in the saddle.

The horse will slam into the ground; its dead fall would have been in the next frame had there been one. My grandfather gets thrown forward with the speed of a projectile. He hits the ground and breaks everything and spends six months in the hospital.

As I stare at the picture, my most intense desire is to rewind a frame so that the characters, horse and rider, can have the leisure of forethought to plan the jump differently.

I pass silver trophies but have no idea where they come from. Later, in a scrapbook I'll spot a photograph of my grandfather in the 1920s, holding one of these same trophies, standing in some long-ago winner's circle with his teammates, surrounded by a crowd shoving to get a better view of the ceremony.

Above: Presentation of the Westchester Cup, 1921. Devereux Milburn, Sr., is at right. Left: Her Majesty the Queen presenting trophy to Hitchcock, Webb, Stevenson, and Milburn, 1927. Below: Tommy Hitchcock blocks Barrett, the number 1 for England, at Hurlingham, 1921.

What impresses me about the scrapbook photographs is the eagerness of the crowd, young and old. Something important has happened and is about to happen, and they want to see.

A trophy from the 1930s sits on a high shelf over the library door. On the walls hang cracked and faded oil paintings of polo horses that were famous in their time.

Commerce where once lay fields and woods makes a hell for wildlife. The animals rub against chain-link fences, skitter across exposed lawns, get mauled on highways.

Deprived of their acreage, the foxes slouch up the hill, pause for a second atop a stone wall across my parents' lawn. I spot them through the bay window of the dining room, beyond a bird feeder owned by bullying blue jays, between branches of a bare apple tree. The austere glow of their eyes.

Lunchtime reality insists they are a couple of foraging dogs, but no breed of dog has so vivid a red coat, or muzzle so sharp. No dog has such a primeval contortion of wariness, heavy scan of head, and spotlit eyes. No dog disappears before your very eyes, creating absence within a space of watchfulness.

In 1992 one estate killed sixteen foxes forced onto its property. They were eating pheasants and ducks and geese, anything to survive.

*Harry Payne Whitney (left) standing
with Major Hardress Lloyd.
Winston Churchill played against
Lloyd in the 1899 Inter-Regimental
Polo Tournament in India.*

Chapter Four

I N T H E I R P R I M E, residents of Old Westbury could get away
with anything. They uprooted enormous trees from Europe, shipped
them over to the States, and had them loaded onto flatbed trucks and
transported out to Long Island. Power cables and telephone lines were
taken down along the route.

It was a time—1913, to be exact—when Harry Payne Whitney, a
noted horse breeder as well as polo player, arrived at Belmont Park on
opening day to watch his two top racehorses, Iron Mask and Whisk
Broom II, compete. That afternoon Belmont Park's ticket sellers staged
a wildcat strike. Ten thousand racing fans milled angrily outside the
grounds. Pinkerton detectives prevented them from scaling the fences
surrounding the track.

Whitney had come to see his horses run. The solution was simple: he
guaranteed admission for all ten thousand racing fans.

IT IS APPROPRIATE to begin modern polo's history at the outset of the
American century. Modern polo is an American game, a power game,
and Harry Payne Whitney invented it. Instead of imitating the English
positional strategies of moving the ball upfield incrementally, man by

man, Whitney favored long passes, hard riding, and continuous switching of positions. He bought only the best horses to match his new breed of sluggers.

Married to a Vanderbilt, Whitney was a rich man accustomed to winning and giving orders. He soon found that not everyone could play his brand of polo. Most American players were locked into the conservative English method, and these habits were hard to break.

Foxhall Keene, considered the most gifted American player of the late 1890s and early 1900s, surrendered his captaincy of the American team to Whitney, while casting a cold eye on the upstart.

"He had a stentorian voice," said Keene of Whitney, "and not only the players but everyone for miles around knew just what he thought. He was in command always, never stopped talking during the game and played the team as though it was a unit obedient to his brain. When he captained a team he worked at it. He kept strict tabs on his players to make sure they kept training rules, chasing [teammates] around London like a headmaster after schoolboys and making sure they got in at a reasonable hour each evening."

Whitney ignored Keene and then dropped him from the American team. He was looking for a different kind of player.

The second piece to the puzzle—in the person of my grandfather— arrived by a circuitous route, one with a violent history that had nothing to do with polo; one that took place thousands of miles from the playing fields of the Hurlingham Club in England.

Had there not been the McKinley assassination in 1901, had the president not decided to stay at the house of his friend John G. Milburn, Whitney would not have been able to put his power team together so quickly, because my grandfather might have played out his career in Buffalo, New York. Whitney needed someone young and strong who could hit the stuffing out of the ball from different angles. Someone who shortened the field with big shots. Someone rough edged, someone who could give the English all kinds of problems.

History intervened and made a short story.

On September 5, 1901, after a leisurely vacation in his beloved hometown of Canton, Ohio, President William McKinley traveled with his wife by private train to Buffalo, New York, to tour the Pan-American Exposition. A Buffalo lawyer named John G. Milburn was president of the exposition and escorted the president.

"Expositions are the timekeepers of progress," said McKinley. Indeed, with its buildings and exhibits from most countries of the Americas, it was attracting visitors at the rate of 116,000 a day.

On the afternoon of September 5, the president spoke before fifty thousand people at the exposition. Much evidence of American progress was on display. Electrical "illuminations" had been created to rival those at the recent Paris exposition. That evening a large and complex fireworks display was mounted. A parade of twenty-two battleships blazed across the night sky; Niagara Falls dripped flame; the very image of the president himself rocketed into the air over a fiery burst of words: "Welcome to McKinley, Chief of Our Nation."

The next day, Friday, September 6, was sweltering. Many spectators carried handkerchiefs. The twenty-eight-year-old anarchist Leon Czolgosz, dressed in a black suit, waited until he was inside the exposition's Temple of Music, shuffling along with the crowd toward the president, before withdrawing from his pocket a snub-nosed .32 caliber Iver Johnson revolver. He calmly wrapped a handkerchief around his gun hand, then mopped his brow visibly with the "injured" hand.

A Secret Service agent tapped Czolgosz on the shoulder, asked if he'd hurt his hand and if he'd care to drop out of line and go to the first-aid station. Czolgosz demurred. "Later," he said. "After I meet the president. I've been waiting a long time."

When Czolgosz reached McKinley, he said, "Excuse my left hand, Mr. President."

President McKinley shook the extended left hand, and Czolgosz moved on. Two other guests shook hands with the president. Then Czolgosz stepped up again and stood three feet from the president. A Secret Service agent named Samuel Ireland grabbed Czolgosz's shoulder to move him along. Czolgosz fired twice through the handkerchief. One bullet glanced off McKinley's breastbone; the other pierced his abdomen.

The president was taken by horse ambulance to the exposition's infirmary, which had a primitive operating room. The abdominal wound was considered the most serious, and a decision was made to operate immediately. The bullet, having passed through the president's stomach and lacerated the front and rear walls, could not be located. Oddly, no use was made of an X-ray machine, even though this new device was one of the attractions at the Buffalo exposition.

After the operation, the president, unconscious and moaning, was taken back to the Milburn house on Delaware Avenue, where he had been staying.

That house became a combination hospital and reception area for dignitaries and members of the administration. The president was dying of gangrene, which slowly retraced the bullet's trail from the inside out, spreading sepsis. No drugs existed to control infection.

His heart weakened, his wife held his hand, then his doctor held his hand, and then he died.

Frank Milburn

A five-minute nationwide gathering of silence on September 21, 1901, marked the beginning of the twentieth century, the beginning of the world as it is. For the first time the diverse strands of the United States were linked by instantaneous communications.

> He usually had a lawbook under his arm in the street and I used to wonder if he was trying to absorb law through his armpits.
>
> —Grover Cleveland on John G. Milburn

He rarely spoke about Czolgosz, the handkerchief, shots, powder burns, or standing next to the president who gushed blood, helping him into a chair.

John G. Milburn was a private man. His home had been invaded by a three-ring circus of politics and death. World attention focused on an ivy-covered mansion that became as famous in its day as the Texas School Book Depository in ours.

Buffalo could no longer be his home. Two years after the assassination, he accepted a job as chief litigator with a prestigious New York City law firm.

He had two sons, John George, Jr., known as George, and Devereux. Both young men had taken up polo while students at Oxford. George Milburn was a good player and reached a handicap of five goals, excellent for his day, a time when the polo association was chary about raising handicaps. At the turn of the century only three polo players in the world were ranked at ten goals.

Devereux Milburn, born in Buffalo in 1881, was a phenomenon. He gave to polo the accurate exertion of enormous physical strength and athletic ability. He was five feet ten inches tall with a leathery face, crinkly black hair, and the arms, shoulders, and chest of a stevedore.

From the beginning Milburn had a clear idea of what he wanted to do. Nothing intimidated him. He had been to college in England, rowed on the Oxford crew against Cambridge, swam on the Oxford swimming team, returned to the United States, graduated from Harvard Law School in 1906, became one of the few graduate students ever admitted to the exclusive Porcellian Club.

Polo made the best use of his skills and strength. He developed a shot called the nearside backhand, which was struck with a scything motion from the rein-hand side of the horse rather than the mallet side. Milburn derived tremendous power from this shot, as much as if he had turned his horse around and hit a forehand.

The nearside backhand is now an integral part of every good polo player's repertoire, though rarely hit with power or used as an offensive weapon. In retrospect, it is amazing that the shot wasn't invented sooner. Perhaps because if the nearside backhand is mis-hit, it can strip all the muscles of a player's back.

This added offensive weapon enabled Milburn to hit a hard shot from either side of the horse. No longer was it necessary to take an extra second to position himself for a backhand. Seconds are precious to a defensive player.

At the turn of the century, polo was as physically demanding as croquet. The British were obsessed with position play. Foursomes of peevish men cantered around in the late afternoon at the Hurlingham Club outside of London to smatterings of applause from the small galleries.

Polo was dying.

When Harry Payne Whitney met Devereux Milburn—who joined the Meadow Brook Club on Long Island in 1906—it was love at first sight.

Above: Devereux Milburn, Sr., on Tenby, his
best horse and one of the best horses in polo for
many years. Below: Spectators at Meadow
Brook Field in the 1920s

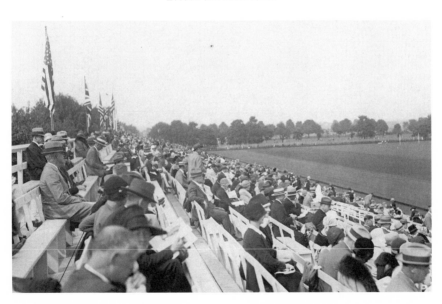

Each felt he had found a man who could implement a new way of playing polo.

Milburn, a nine-goal player at the age of twenty-five, was the missing ingredient that the American team needed. Since it was Whitney's ball, so to speak—he had the money and the horses—it was up to him to select the American four that would play in England in 1909. That team became known as the Big Four—Larry and Monty Waterbury, Harry Payne Whitney, Devereux Milburn.

Milburn regarded his own back, or defensive, position as a unique vantage point for launching offensive sallies. This tactic put pressure on the other team by bringing four men instead of three to bear on the opponent's goal. Since Milburn could hit a backhand the length of the field, it also freed the number 1 or 2 player to gallop ahead of the pack. An offensive threat by the opposition could immediately turn into an offensive threat by Whitney's team.

One more thing: the American game worked only when players rode the best horses available. Making full use of the 12.4-acre polo field required enormous stamina from horse and rider.

The American version was exciting and dangerous. When a man or woman hit the ground in the power game, the horse was traveling at thirty-five miles per hour, and bad things happened. The rider bounced along the turf; the horse fell on the rider; the rider got run over by players in hot pursuit; or the rider bailed out, breaking his legs.

Milburn cared nothing for the rarefied social associations of polo. For him the game was hockey on horseback. Players sweated, got their uniforms dirty, and at the end of the day knew they'd been in a game.

Harry Payne Whitney was a boisterous presence and natural leader. He had the organizational skills of a field marshal, which he needed to move horses, men, grooms, and families and to find stables and housing three thousand miles away in England for the Westchester Cup.

Milburn and Whitney's hell-for-leather game put a charge into the sport. It was so exuberant, so . . . American. Nobody had seen anything like it.

The Americans defeated the British in 1909, 1911, and 1913. Each time the scores were a little closer. The British adjusted, and by 1913 the Americans won the Westchester Cup by only one-fourth of a goal. (Scoring was different then, with half and quarter goals sometimes awarded on fouls.)

In 1914 Whitney retired from international polo (though he stayed ranked at ten goals for several more years). He left three of the original Big Four to tangle with a superb British foursome. Joining the Waterburys and Milburn was a competent six-goaler named Rene La Montagne, Jr.

It would have taken the Big Four intact and at the top of its game in 1914 to have had any chance to retain the Westchester Cup. The final score of the second game of the 1913 championships had been the United States 4½, England 4¼, which remains the closest match in international polo history. The English were on their way to reasserting a superiority they had lost after 1902, when the Americans began to dominate. They had the men and the horses to do it.

Milburn got married in 1913. As a wedding present Harry Payne Whitney gave him his six best polo horses and his best groom.

The Americans made two costly mistakes in 1914. They split up the Waterburys, who were the best brother combination in the history of polo and always played in tandem at the 1 and 2 positions, and they moved Milburn out of his customary back position to play number 3.

Whether this was Milburn's idea or not, I don't know. It was like asking a catcher to pitch the seventh game of a World Series. He was dreadful. The scores were 8½–3 and 4–2¾.

When I was very young, I read a book called *The Tumult and the Shouting*, a memoir published in the 1950s by the sportswriter Grantland Rice. Rice is best known for his poem "Alumnus Football," which has the lines, "When the One Great Scorer comes to write against your name— / He marks—not that you won or lost—but how you played the game." Rice also wrote famously of an Army–Notre Dame football game: "Outlined against a blue-gray October sky rode the Four Horsemen . . ."

Rice's overripe prose style was suited to the outsized events of the golden age of sports and, better yet, to a child's hungry imagination. His memoir has a chapter entitled "The Two Horsemen, Hitchcock and Milburn." Rice felt closer to Milburn than Hitchcock because they were approximately the same age, while Hitchcock was quite a bit younger. Rice summed up their characters this way: "I believe Hitchcock would charge headlong into a two-pronged, raging rhinoceros if the critter blocked his path. Milburn would first ask it to move."

I loved this description. I imagined the Kipling jungle and that pawing rhino—Hitchcock charging gleefully, Milburn polite.

What I want to get at here is that my grandfather had the time of his life, even though the 1914 matches were a disaster. It didn't matter to him that his team lost or that he played out of position. The important thing was that both teams charged up and down the field in raw displays of power polo. The best team won, and that was that.

Those two years, 1913 and 1914, were the real golden age of polo. Milburn played into the 1930s and never found such caliber of opponents again.

The year 1914 marked the end of fun for him, or, more accurately, the end of great fun. There is a note of lament when he tells Rice over and over, a quarter century after the event, "Cheape was riding for them then. . . ."

Leslie Cheape, the best English player of the prewar era, and one of the best players who ever lived, defined the number 1 position and was also superb at 2. He and Milburn battled each other up and down the field, just for those two years, five matches in all.

As a child I did not understand, after reading Rice's chapter, how the Americans could have so much fun and still lose. I didn't understand that they simply might not care, just as long as the game was good.

The cream of British polo did not survive the war. Besides Cheape, three other top British players were killed. Rivy Grenfell died in the trenches; his brother Francis was posthumously awarded the Victoria Cross, the first British soldier to be so honored in World War I.

Noel Edwards, who played number 2 for the British team in 1913, became one of the first British officers killed by gas.

I have beside me a photograph of Edwards upon the happy greensward. My grandfather gallops behind him on a white horse. The grandstand is packed with ten or fifteen thousand fans. The year must be 1913. A larky time frozen. Edwards has just hit a backhand. I note the clarity, the impressive size of the field. That's what always gets me about polo—its antiquated spaciousness. A spectator easily gets lost in the space.

The British were never the same. Throughout the twenties and thirties the Americans defeated them by scores of 15–3 or 12–2, pure routs. Milburn told Grantland Rice that it was so boring, year after year, eleven goals ahead, cantering up and down the field. The effort was not to win but to stay awake.

Milburn fought in the war, too. He came home to play polo and practice law at Carter, Ledyard & Milburn on Wall Street. He built a house in Old Westbury, married Nancy Steele, the daughter of Charles Steele, a J. P. Morgan partner. Steele had a nine-hole golf course and a special cabin built solely for washing his dogs. He had butlers and footmen, made annual trips to Scotland to blast away on the moors.

I believe Milburn would have quit polo after 1914, with nobody left to play against, and perhaps have devoted his weekends to recreational golf or tennis. That is, had it not been for the arrival of polo's Babe Ruth, the man who gave the sport the kind of indefinable glamorous aura craved by Americans in the 1920s—our first age of celebrity.

LACONIC, BUSINESSLIKE, immensely strong, Tommy Hitchcock methodically went about his play on a polo field. After the game he headed home. He didn't make small talk, never lingered to rehash the afternoon's match over Southsides in the grill room at the Meadow Brook Club. He treated his horses like machines, didn't extol them. They were transportation.

He was conceited; he was modest; he was distant; he was voluble. He had complexity. A lot of people liked him and a lot of people didn't. I consider him the toughest athletic competitor of this century. Milburn, who threw around compliments like they were steel girders, thought Hitchcock should have been ranked at twelve goals.

My grandfather had a genius on his hands, and he knew it. They made a great team: the aging power back, pushing forty, still strong and canny, and this amazing young talent, twenty-one years old when he burst onto the international polo scene.

Unfortunately, the first thing Milburn did, as captain of the 1921 U.S. four playing for the Westchester Cup in England, was to throw

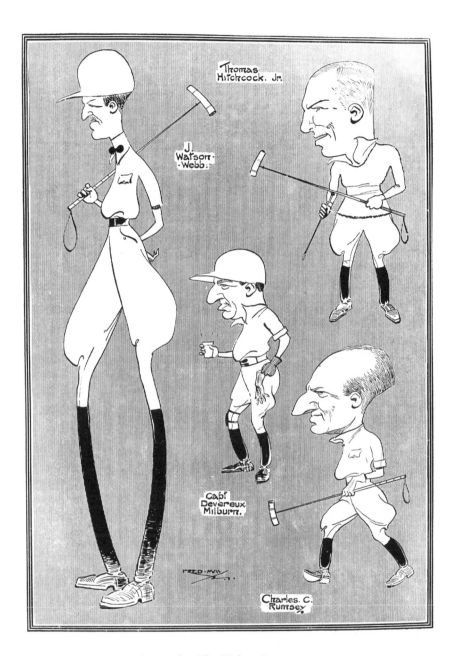

Cartoon from The Tatler, *August 6, 1921*

Hitchcock off the team. The reasons are obscure. Perhaps hobnobbing with the cream of British aristocracy and royalty interfered with the great man's concentration. The suspension didn't last long, and it was the last time anyone removed Tommy Hitchcock from a polo team.

Cut away the integuments of polo—its high-life image, its princes and maharajas and sultans who swat the ball—and the game is revealed in simplicity. Polo is many sports in one, with elements of hockey, baseball, tennis, soccer, wild elements of the cowboy, ranches, and cutting horses. Of cavalry feats of horsemanship that border on trick riding. Spectators often complain that the field is too big, the action too far away, but they would not complain if they saw better polo.

They had something, those first of the modern polo players. They had class. A story in *Polo* magazine reminds us of this.

During World War II Hitchcock had been in the Army Air Corps, stationed briefly in Australia. An Aussie officer, with a pronounced dislike of Americans—one of those "overpaid, oversexed, and over here" reactions, presumably—wrote to *Polo* to say that he had made friends with Hitchcock during the war and enclosed a photograph of the American with his unit. He also mentioned his surprise that at no time during their friendship did Hitchcock ever mention that he played polo. The Aussie found Hitchcock courteous, competent, knowledgeable about his aviation duties, modest.

When a friend of the Aussie happened to mention to him that Hitchcock played polo, the Aussie asked, "Is he any good?"

Hitchcock was dead at forty-four. As a test pilot stationed in England during World War II, he took up a problem-ridden Mustang, radioed the tower that he had located and solved the problem but had found another one. Moments later, his plane plunged into Salisbury Plain.

Frank Milburn

. . .

POLO WAS front-page news in 1921. People were much closer to the age of the horse than to the age of the automobile. It was news when, just before the start of the 1921 Westchester Cup against England at Hurlingham, Milburn sprained his back, forcing him to cancel lunch with the king.

The Americans asked for an extension until he recovered. The English polo association refused. This was not sporting. The Americans had delayed the 1914 Westchester Cup at Meadow Brook so Leslie Cheape could recuperate from a broken nose suffered when it got mashed by a polo ball. The English were not sporting, perhaps, but wise. They were outgunned; the absence of Milburn would make things more even.

The king's physician was summoned to attend Milburn. His word would be final. The doctor allowed him to play. Between periods Milburn wrapped himself in a heavy rug to prevent his muscles from tightening. On the field he showed no effects of the injury, and the Americans romped.

In 1921, 1924, and 1927, the Americans had the greatest polo team ever assembled. J. Watson Webb at number 1 was a brilliant strategist and the only left-handed player in polo. (Later, the rules banned left-handers entirely, because it was believed they inadvertently caused dangerous fouls.)

At number 2 rode Tommy Hitchcock, the master. At number 3 was either Louis Stoddard or Malcolm Stevenson, both top-ranked players. Stoddard had terrific horses. At number 4 was Milburn, still good even though nudging fifty.

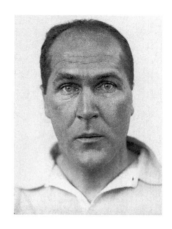

Above left: Devereux Milburn, Sr., 1927
Above right: Malcolm Stevenson, 1927
Below: The 1927 American team, from left to
right: Milburn, Stevenson, Hitchcock, Webb.
Note that Webb played left-handed, which
would be illegal today.

When judged by their photographs, this team was extremely intimidating physically. They looked craggy, dour, banged up, and not gentlemanly. Webb resembled a hanging judge; the rest of the team stared out as if looking for a rope.

> No sport, save possibly steeplechasing and football, is so good a school in this respect as polo. This element of personal risk is not a drawback but a decided advantage. No matter how brave a man may be he is none the less a creature of habit. If his most lethal experience prior to battle has consisted in dodging automobiles on city streets the insinuating whisper of bullets about his sacred person will have a more disquieting influence on him than would be the case had the same person received a few cuts and broken bones on the polo field.
>
> —Captain George S. Patton, 1906

(General George S. Patton was an avid poloist. As a young cavalry officer stationed in Hawaii in the 1920s, he took several bad falls in games. These resulted in severe concussions, but he still couldn't get enough polo. Historians speculate that the head injuries were the origins of Patton's mood swings and eccentric behavior. All those brave Patton troops, as Paul Fussell has pointed out in his book *Wartime*, who died in the European theater with their neckties neatly tied.)

MY GRANDFATHER owned a brown English gelding named Tenby, who was the best horse in polo at the time. Tenby had a problem—he wouldn't stop. Sometimes Milburn stopped, but the horse didn't. He once fell off Tenby three times in a period.

Milburn would offer Tenby to other players for a period or two, but while everyone knew the horse was great, they also knew he had this important quirk and declined the offer. Milburn rode Tenby for three periods in the 1921 championships—just as he had in 1913 and 1914—which was a tribute to the eighteen-year-old horse's talent and endurance.

On the voyage back to the States, Tenby died of natural causes. He was accorded a full shipboard funeral. Prayers were offered; the great horse was draped with an American flag. My father, four years old in 1921, recalls Tenby sliding into the sea from under the flag. Ungainly dead weight and froth. It was one of his earliest memories.

> In this second game [of the 1927 Westchester Cup, won by the Americans] occurred one of those fine acts of sportsmanship that so frequently stand out in these matches between England and America.
>
> With several periods to play and the game anybody's, Mr. [Malcolm] Stevenson was hurt by a flying ball which caught him squarely in the kneecap, paralyzing temporarily his whole left leg. Painfully hurt, he came back into the game at the end of some ten or fifteen minutes and was met by Captain George with an inquiry as to which leg was the injured one. On being told, the English player pulled around and throughout the desperately played remainder of the game, in spite of the important advantage that was his, never once bumped or rode Stevenson off on his near side.
>
> —Newell Bent, *American Polo*

I have kept that painting of my grandfather with me all these years.

Between periods. A chestnut polo pony named Gargantilla, white at the throat, is prancing with neck held high. A groom, formal in brown breeches and shiny boots, holds a fresh horse called Sunbeam. The groom's name is McCullough. He was part of the 1913 wedding gift from Harry Payne Whitney.

My grandfather's mallet is raised like a half-unsheathed sword. In moments he will ride out to the field in the background, shadows of players, teammates, and opponents.

Devereux Milburn wears a robin's-egg-blue shirt and white breeches,

Above: Tommy Hitchcock, c. 1930
Left: James Watson Webb, 1927

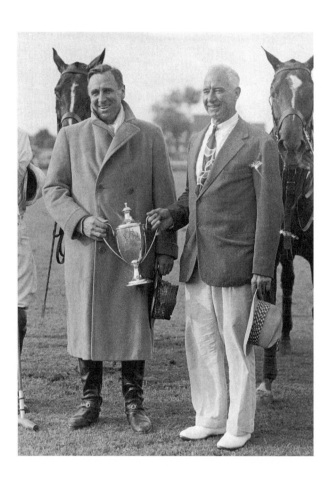

*Devereux Milburn, Sr., presenting a trophy
to Tommy Hitchcock, 1939*

the colors of Meadow Brook. He looks both formidable and secure in the saddle. Horse and rider are outsized, blocking, difficult to get by. From fitted helmet to bulging forearm, he gives an impression of unyielding strength.

He looks pristine and unbruised, as if the sport he played were antiseptic. Just a rich guy cantering around, rarely breaking a sweat. Artistic license, an exalted image. In the painting his collar is starched. There is no sound and fury. Steel pins holding him together are not visible.

In 1930 my grandfather was forty-nine years old. The last of his major polo battles had taken place three years earlier. He had already played on seven American teams against England for the Westchester Cup (1909, 1911, 1913, 1914, 1921, 1924, and 1927) and had captained the 1921, 1924, and 1927 teams.

Perhaps in the 1920s, had there been no Great War, matches between England and the United States would have solidified polo in the American consciousness. One can only dream about duels between Tommy Hitchcock and Leslie Cheape or wonder what would have happened if the Grenfell twins had survived the war.

The 1920s became the Age of Hitchcock, followed in the mid-1930s by the Age of Argentina, which has continued to this day. Argentina has not lost an international polo championship since 1932. With the America's Cup in sailing having changed hands in recent years, Argentina's national polo team may have the longest undefeated record in modern sports.

Hitchcock went on to further greatness. The best polo players every year, male and female, are awarded Tommys at ceremonies in Florida. The award is a bronze statuette of Tommy Hitchcock.

Long after my grandfather retired from championship polo, he watched Hitchcock play in the finals of the 1935 U.S. Open, and declared, "I have never seen anyone play like that—anywhere!" This, from someone who had watched them all since 1902. In the semifinals Hitchcock struck a ball in midair and smashed it ninety yards ahead for a goal. The man and the sport were one.

Only in great international matches did Hitchcock ride the best horses. At no time in his career was he particularly well mounted—unlike, say, Averell Harriman or Laddie Sanford, who had inherited vast fortunes. It is a tribute to his consummate skill that he played always at the top level.

"Cheape was riding for them then. . . ."

CRUSADER

In Memoriam—Leslie St. Clair Cheape

Duty impelled you, and you never faltered—
There was no need for her to whisper twice;
The end you saw not—no, nor would have altered—
You took the cross, and made the sacrifice.
        —Unknown

"Mr. Thomas Hitchcock, Jr., was recently described by a fellow internationalist [that is, Milburn] as the 'only man, with the exception of the late Captain Leslie Cheape, able to play any of the four positions on a polo team and be worth ten goals in each of the four places.' "

A word about Leslie Cheape, though sad. I can almost hear my grandfather from across the decades saying, "The pity."

An English writer of the time, A. S. Barrow, described him:

He was not only the best polo horseman that we have seen for at least two decades, but the best exponent of the fast game, which is the only kind which counts when first-class polo is under discussion. It was Leslie Cheape's perception of the essential which, since the war [World War I] seems to have been forgotten—high speed and accurate shooting—which made him the great player that he was, and has caused him to be the model, to which all who aspire to first-class honors must work. It may be said that with the International Team of 1914 in which Leslie Cheape played No. 2, the art of fast polo died in England. The great thing about Leslie was his wonderful accuracy, and the terrific drive he could get on his shots. They left the ground like bullets out of a gun, and they were usually in the right direction.

He was born on October 5, 1882. His mother was a noted sportswoman (as was Hitchcock's). His father, a lieutenant colonel in the Tenth Hussars, was one of the officers at Aldershot who played in the first polo match in England in 1869.

Leslie Cheape learned his polo with the cavalry in India and by 1911 was clearly marked for international play. Quite simply, he dominated the center of a polo field. On Easter Sunday, 1916, as an officer in the Worcestershire Yeomanry, he was bivouacked near the Suez Canal in Egypt at a nowhere town called Oglertina. Wrote a colleague, Charles J. Coventry, colonel in the Worcestershire Yeomanry, of the absurd, tragic events amid a literal fog of war:

There had been no report of the presence of an enemy from airplane observation, other than a band of sixty camel men who were constantly bothering us, and they [Cheape's men] felt quite secure. A very heavy fog indeed came down that night, and early in the morning about 6:30 I think, it was reported to Thomas [a squadron commander] that a party of camels were drinking at our wells. It was too thick with the fog to see anything, but Thomas consulted with Leslie, and they came

*Leslie Cheape in the center, pursued
by Harry Payne Whitney in white, 1913.
It is regrettable that so few pictures of
Cheape exist.*

to the conclusion that they had better fire on this party, which was accordingly done. It turned out to be a most awful mistake, as the party they heard was in reality the rear guard of the Turkish force, the main body having slipped by in the darkness and fog, never knowing that Oglertina was occupied. This mistake was no one's fault, and no blame could possibly be attached to any of our men. However, having once opened fire the Turks realized that they would have to take Oglertina before going on to Katia, and they formed up for an attack. The fog was so dense that nothing could be seen, and Thomas and Leslie had to dispose of their squadrons as best they could. They had no means of knowing, nor did they realize that the strength of the Turkish Army was about 6,000, otherwise they might have got away, if they had at once made up their minds to do so; and then a little later it was too late; for though they might have galloped off themselves, they had a party of sixty dismounted engineers with them and they naturally could not leave them behind. The Turks got all around them, and soon it was practically a hand-to-hand fight. Thomas and Leslie were consulting together, and Leslie had just turned away to go back to his section, when he was shot, and Thomas told me that he never moved. All were heroes that day and covered themselves with glory. It may also interest you to know that whilst marching to Makabra I was riding with Brigadier General Wiggin, and he told me to fill in a list of honors for good work done in the desert, and I told him that I should put forward the names of my three squadron leaders for special mention, and hoped they would get the D.S.O. This, of course, included Leslie. Again on my return home I put forth Thomas' and Leslie's names for the D.S.O. in connection with the engagement at Oglertina. They granted it to Thomas but would give no posthumous honors. Leslie, besides being all he was privately, was a really fine soldier in every way.

A handful of people are alive who saw him play. I would have liked to re-create Captain Leslie Cheape archivally, unearthing the minutes and color of his games. But vital polo records—the entire history of the sport, really—were destroyed by fire during World War II when the

Hurlingham Club, polo's historical repository, was bombed into rubble.

When my grandfather said, "Cheape was riding for them then," he was speaking of a master. More important, his readers knew what he was talking about. A public tradition existed. Now it is necessary to reinvent polo for the public, as one would reinvent arcane sports like court tennis, racquets, or roque.

When Devereux Milburn retired from polo no one else at defense could backhand the ball to Hitchcock with power and accuracy. Hitchcock shifted from the 2 to 3 position, where he played out his career. He was still the best, but he was not the genius at 3 that he had been at 2. He admitted as much. He was primarily a great hitter of the ball, which is what the 2 position is about. The 3 player customarily pivots between offense and defense. As the playmaker, 3 studies his troops arrayed, makes passes ahead, or drops back on defense. The assessive hesitation of leadership was not fundamentally Hitchcock's style.

At 3 Hitchcock had company in greatness—whether Harry Payne Whitney of the prewar era; Cecil Smith, the genial hard-hitting Texan and ten-goal player for twenty-five straight years; Bob Skene, the Australian wizard; or, in the 1960s and 1970s, the lordly Juan Carlos Harriott of Argentina.

Grantland Rice's chapter on Milburn and Hitchcock became not a literary but a physical artifact. Yes, they really had lived, and someone had written them down.

I read how one winter afternoon my grandfather drove over to the Meadow Brook Club and played eighteen holes in the snow. On the first tee, according to Rice, he produced a bag of red golf balls and drove down a white fairway into a wall of bitter wind. Hooking a drive into snowy woods, he tramped around for twenty minutes looking for the ball. He knocked his next shot onto the green, or, to paraphrase Wallace Stevens, not onto the green but where the green might be.

He was more interested in losing well than winning badly. He never pointed fingers or made excuses. Blame would have been unthinkable to him. He won with a team and lost with a team and played with the players he had been dealt. If he or they didn't measure up, as in 1914, that did not in the least dilute his pleasure.

It seems to me that he got the maximum fun that sports can offer—existential, of the moment, inside the game, with thoughts of outcome suspended.

ONE MORE THING about that painting of my grandfather. There is the young groom McCullough holding Sunbeam. He wears a formal brown suit, disassociated from sweat and leather and horse manure.

I never knew McCullough's first name. He stayed on long after my grandfather died, continuing as head groom through most of my father's polo career and my childhood. He was old then, talked to himself, had a way of soothing horses by making soft blubbery sounds through his lips as he saddled or groomed them. This was decades after the great international matches and crowds of forty thousand. Now a hundred people might show up. No special trains were scheduled by the Long Island Rail Road anymore. Polo is dull unless played well.

The spectators had once been brought out by the quality of games—intimate engagements, heroic, romantic, warlike without war. This was a time when cavalry still carried the battle, sabers flashed—not the hideous world of trenches, mustard gas, and long-range artillery.

For a brief age, here was a sport people couldn't get anywhere else. In polo there is no tranquillity of movement as in baseball or cricket; nowhere to rest the peaceful eye. A well-played game makes astonishing demands of spectator and player alike because high-speed teamwork and split-second decisions are required.

There is a bronze sculpture of the Big Four—Whitney, two Waterburys, and Milburn—by Herbert Haseltine. It stands in the lobby of the Racquet & Tennis Club in New York. The sculpture is beautiful—Haseltine's specialty was horses—and has been reproduced many times.

Harry Payne Whitney leads the Big Four into battle. His horse rears, and he points his mallet like a sword, encouraging his troops onward. Whitney was a loudmouth, but it was his energy and volubly expressed ideas that brought the sport out of the Victorian age.

In the Haseltine sculpture, Whitney is followed by the Waterbury brothers. Milburn brings up the rear. Haseltine has given him a precombat meditative quality, gentle and tired. His horse's head is down, with its neck slightly elongated. His mallet-weapon rests across the horse's withers in a benign, nonthreatening position. His shoulders are slumped, his head pushed downward slightly.

For a long time I thought that my grandfather was out of synchronization with the rest of his teammates. They were leading a charge onto the field to begin the game, the boisterous Americans, but Devereux Milburn looked as if he had finished eight periods of a brutal championship. Later, I came to realize what horse and rider showed vividly: the wear and tear of experience hard won.

Part Two

Geoffrey Kent, third from left,
with Prince Charles after a game
at the Guards Polo Club

Chapter Five

I<small>N THE</small> 1990s being one of polo's heavy hitters can cost a million dollars a year. A top professional player will earn about that much as well.

A man with disposable income must hire a professional player or players, usually Argentinean, to play with him on his team. This man, called a patron, is often told politely by the professional not to touch the ball for the duration of the game. Polo is a sport in which it is necessary to worry about getting killed. One patron, for example, is more than eighty years old and regularly hires nine-goal Argentineans in their twenties to play on his team.

Often the patron spends hot afternoons cantering around the field while the real action takes place a hundred yards or more away from him. If he does get a chance to hit the ball, a professional teammate will be galloping directly behind him, yelling, "Leave it! Leave it!" This is shouted at a man who is accustomed to deference in real life.

When the professional shouts "Leave it!" the ball must be left. This rule is the oldest in the sport, going back to the ancient Persians.

I<small>T IS IMPOSSIBLE</small> to discuss contemporary polo without mentioning Prince Charles, the world's most famous player—and a good one. He lacks a hard shot but compensates with accuracy. He also recognizes that, because of polo's high speeds, hitting the ball only one yard can reverse the flow of play.

The prince performs unglamorous but necessary work away from the ball—riding off his opponent, covering his position. His Highness is not afraid to mix it up. Teammates and opponents carefully call him "sir," even in the heat of action, and even though he is not a patron.

Henry James wrote from Lamb House that the most beautiful phrase in the English language is "summer afternoon." It is pleasant to envision polo as a game of a few friends gathered on a late-summer afternoon to ride around, work up a sweat, yell at each other, and go home.

The best of the English see polo that way, too—summer afternoons and then a pint or a Pimm's back at the clubhouse. These English polo players believe in a democracy of the playing fields. Always a drink with teammates after the game—a rugbylike mateyness, a dropping of the guard, a momentary forgetfulness about titles, a sharing with their natural leader.

What I like best about English polo is its informality. The English make a gospel of dressing down, ambling over and happening to encounter a polo match—found objects racing across the grass. They sit in rickety grandstands and have a look and then wander away again in their worn brown Barbours, holding furled professional-looking umbrellas; sauntering onto the field at halftime to replace divots, give their dogs a run, plunge their hands deep in their pockets as they chat.

There is never any sense of event about English polo games. One goes, sits down, observes, moves on, wanders among the pony lines, points out a good shot amid smatterings of applause.

The Prince of Wales seems to catch that spirit, too. He arrives at games in his sports car, accompanied by a bodyguard, gets out, changes his shirt, mounts his horse, and is gone out to the field for practice before the game. He has no motorcade, no entourage, and no particular small talk—he is just another player. Sometimes he makes a joke and sometimes not, and sometimes he looks as if he isn't having a good time.

During his pregame preparations photographs of him are not permitted. A policeman will walk over to any raised camera and say, "Sorry, sir, no pictures." I think this has to do with photographing the prince bare chested, a pose that has appeared in some tabloids and is considered undignified.

The closer one gets to a celebrity, the less impressive he is, the more a human factor accounts. Once when the prince walked by on his gray horse, I almost called out, "How's it going?" but stifled myself—so remarkably average did he appear to be.

At all times the prince is hovered over and succored by Major Ronald Ferguson, his polo manager and the father of the Duchess of York. A player himself, Ferguson has a military bearing and startling red, bushy, look-of-eagles eyebrows.

One day I watched the prince play back for the Windsor Park team. Windsor Castle floated in the misty distance beyond the fields. The patron of the team was an affable, handsome, Kenya-born four-goaler named Geoffrey Kent, the founder of Abercrombie & Kent, a luxury travel company that he had started from nothing and turned into a great success. Elegant African camera safaris were their specialty.

Kent was married to the former Jorie Butler, a woman whose father, the late Paul Butler, had been one of American polo's driving forces, for nearly half a century, especially in the Midwest. For many years the United States Open was played at Butler's Oak Brook polo club outside of Chicago.

When I saw him play, Kent was an excellent number 1, had speedy horses, and knew what to do with the ball when it got passed up to him. He told me that his great regret was taking up polo so late in life, in his midthirties. He sounded nostalgic for what might have been, but being ranked at four goals was pretty good for a man who had been playing polo for only eight or nine years.

On this late-June afternoon, Kent's Windsor Park team, with the Prince of Wales playing defense, was opposed by the Maple Leafs, whose patron was a Canadian billionaire named Galen Weston. Weston had recently purchased Fort Belvedere on the estate of Windsor Park. It had once been the home of the Duke of Windsor, the abdicated Edward VIII. A tall, thin, remote man, Weston had also recently bought Fortnum & Mason, the London specialty store.

The game was not precisely to my taste. With the prince playing, and with the Duchess of York—Fergie—on hand to present the trophy, there was an air of formality and celebrity, abetted by the casts of the television shows "Dynasty" and "Hill Street Blues"—John Forsythe, Linda Evans, Veronica Hamel—who were on a charity junket through England, sponsored by Reebok.

Impeccably tailored corporate types sipped champagne under a striped VIP tent. Four or five hundred people filled the small grandstand as the game got under way. The afternoon was overcast, with a seeping chill. In such weather the mildest head cold might linger for weeks.

Three things were interesting about that game. First, the crowd was utterly baffled. Most didn't know a thing about polo, and the game confused them. They couldn't tell a bad play from a good one, and after a while turned away to talk among themselves.

Second, there was a terrible fall in the middle of the game. The crowd reacted as if the accident were theater or a movie in which the horse goes down, and the cowboy with it, but of course it is only make-believe, and horse and rider will get up from the ground and play on.

This time the horse got up, but the player didn't. He lay there, and an ambulance was summoned. His wife ran onto the field and stood over him, and it was serious because he didn't move. One of the Maple Leafs.

The player's name was Julian Hipwood, a nine-goaler and perhaps the best of the English professionals. The reason Hipwood was not ranked at ten goals was that he had a tendency to overdrive his lights, to perform everything at full speed, even when slowing down would have been prudent.

As if recognizing his own unique way of playing, Hipwood was the only professional polo player I saw in England, Argentina, or the United States who wore a crash helmet. A rugged man with the build of a rugby player, in this game he had been racing after a shot at full tilt when his horse stumbled. Hipwood went flying and then bounced and rolled along the ground for fifteen yards, came to a stop floppily, and lay motionless.

This was a Hipwood specialty; he crashed frequently. I have a photograph of him lying under a horse that has fallen on top of him. Only his knee and a flipper of hand peek out between horse and grass. He walked away from that one, too.

Hipwood staggered up from this accident, but the game was over for him. The mask of his crash helmet had sliced his face. Plump blood streaks made him look as if he were being bled by leeches.

Later, when I encountered Hipwood in the Guards Polo Club bar, he had no idea where he was. His wife guided him from chair to chair as he sought relief from his injuries. His eyes were glassy, and he lurched.

The third thing that impressed me was how, as the Duchess of York presented trophies to the teams after the game, a white handkerchief appeared miraculously in the hand of the Prince of Wales, whereupon he wiped his nose. The handkerchief appeared as a kind of deus ex machina, thrust to him in the blink of an eye. First, the prince rubbed his nose lightly and the next instant patted his nose with a handkerchief. Someone must have handed it to him—his bodyguard perhaps—with a celerity bordering on the invisible, because I had been observing the prince the whole time in my reportorial capacity.

It's a small thing, I know, wiping one's nose, but I thought it was totally royal—the speed-of-light anticipation of his need.

This sort of polo—full of celebrities, nobody in the stands knowing what was going on, and everybody dressed up, the women's high heels sucked into the gentle turf as they struggled womanfully to replace divots at halftime—well, reinforced polo's fatal image as a sport accompanied by the incessant popping of champagne corks.

IN ENGLAND, though, I discovered a very different place at Cowdray Park, a few hours south of London. There is almost always a polo game in progress; the fans are knowledgeable, the land stunning: deep woods, winding trails, rolling hills, meandering streams. Polo fields conform to the land, and not vice versa, as if the fields had been laid down just that day with a gentle carpeting, a silent rolling meadowland, in order not to cause a disturbance.

Cowdray Park comprises many thousands of acres and is owned by Lord Cowdray, one of the wealthiest men in England, a former polo player himself who lost an arm in World War II but kept playing through the 1950s. Some find his self-effacement trying in a man of such prominence, but Cowdray Park reflects a taste for discovery and for the informality of gorgeous natural parkland. The polo fields are unboarded,

Above: Lord Cowdray, 1930
Below: Spreading out the field at Cowdray
Park, with the famed castle ruins in the
background

adding to the meadow feeling—unboarded because years ago a friend of Lord Cowdray's had been crushed to death against the boards.

Sadly, friends told me that seemingly from one day to the next Lord Cowdray had gone from hale to frail. They traced his decline to the vicious windstorm of October 1987, which wreaked destruction across southern England. Lord Cowdray lost thousands of trees on his parkland—uprooted, flung in numbers wholesale and so large that a mind cannot conceive it. One forest of beloved pines was mowed down to smithereens as the storm moved with a tornado's force across his green world. Many sad uprootings are still visible beside delicate traceries of roads.

Cowdray Park was the headquarters of the Hurlingham Polo Association, a venerable institution more than a century old. I expected the club to be a large porticoed edifice overlooking the most beautiful polo fields in the world. It had once been the scene of magnificent international championships. Indeed, I had built the club into mythical proportions, invented aged colonels sitting on the veranda reminiscing about army polo in India under the Raj.

That world has not only vanished, it has been obliterated. What time didn't do, the Luftwaffe accomplished during World War II, bombing the club into rubble. All that remained of the game's history was housed in a small brick building behind the house of the Hurlingham Club's secretary, Colonel A. W. Harper: a few hundred books at most, their bindings blackened from the fire that destroyed the club's polo library.

Still, it was a pleasure to sit in that musty one-room cottage and leaf through what history remained. I studied the minutes of games one hundred years old. Flaking polo magazines of the 1920s had advertisements recommending a cup of coffee before bedtime to ensure tranquil sleep.

Also extolled were the health-giving properties of cigarettes. On the shelves I came across an account of the career of Rao Rajah Hanut Singh in J.N.P. Watson's invaluable *The World of Polo* (Boston, 1986). There is no better exemplar of Indian polo than Hanut Singh, surely one of the greatest players who ever lived. His career spanned the first sixty-five years of this century; from the glory days of the twenties and thirties to the early 1960s, when he underwent a personal polo renaissance on English playing fields. He carried on an Indian polo tradition that put as much emphasis on cerebral strategy as on brute physical strength.

Hanut Singh was born in 1900, and learned polo from his sportsman father and the best Indian players of the time. He served with the Jodhpur Lancers in World War I. Within two years after his return to India, he was ranked at nine goals, a handicap he retained until 1939.

He was good enough to play on English teams against America for the Hurlingham Cup during his prime, but the Hurlingham polo committee decided that he was a lightweight, too small to compete against the burly Americans. In retrospect, this seems like a dreadful mistake, since the English were shorthanded after World War I—so many killed. Singh played longer than anyone in polo history, retiring, finally, with a three-goal handicap at the age of seventy-two. "I could have slipped them [the Americans] every time. My ponies were so fast and handy."

In 1936 he was finally invited to compete in the Westchester matches, but he was injured and couldn't play.

In 1970 Hanut Singh recounted for Watson what he regarded as the greatest match he played in during a long and eventful career. Something of the pride in his considerable abilities comes through in his words, as well as a little of the sense of a vanished age when Indian polo could not be matched for sheer glamour.

Above: A parade of Indian polo ponies and grooms at Meadow Brook. Below: Hanut Singh, second from left, with the Maharaja of Jaipur, second from right, and Singh's sons Harri, far left, and Bijai, far right. The lady presenting the trophy at Cowdray Park is unknown.

Even after all those wonderful years of international polo, I would still choose as my greatest game a contest which took place almost 50 years ago in India.

It was in 1922 during a visit to India by the Prince of Wales, himself a keen polo player. He offered a cup for a tournament held in his honour. The final was between my team, Jodhpur, and a team we had never beaten, the great Patiala [ranked at 36 goals], which had won everything up until the First World War and was still unbeaten after the war.

Imagine the scene in Delhi: a crowd of 150,000 [this number cannot be verified, but a crowd of 100,000 would not be an exaggeration] around the polo field, among them the future King of England, the Viceroy, some 50 maharajas and princes, dozens of generals and high government officials and all the ladies dressed as if they were to be received at Court. Such an atmosphere naturally added to our determination to win. My father [Sir Pertarb Singh] had set his heart on this game and we had a string of 150 ponies from which to choose. Patiala had even greater resources, including a style of polo that I can only describe as a chess game, a wonderful control of the ball from all corners of the field. We knew the only way to beat them was with a game of speed, always playing the ball to an imaginary line straight down the centre of the field from one goal to another. That is the way we played, but Patiala was still leading 4–0 in the third chukka. I finally scored just before the interval, and after the interval we caught fire, drawing even with Patiala and, in the final minute of the match, passing them. The roars from the crowd were so deafening that none of us heard the final bugle and we knew the game was over only when thousands of spectators began pouring onto the field. As my No. 1, Prithi Singh, rode past the V.I.P. pavilion, he swung his stick round and round his head and threw it high into the air. Dignitaries from the pavilion rushed out onto the field to capture the stick as a souvenir. It was a scene I will never forget, but what I remember most was the reaction of my father, who died later that year. I think Sir H. Perry-Robinson, writing in the Times of London, described the end of the game better than I can. "Halfway through the chukka Jodhpur scored and drew even at five-all. Three more minutes to go, and through those minutes men, important major-generals and personages in high political office, stood up in the grandstand waving their hats and shouting themselves hoarse, and women screamed. Only one figure it seems sat motionless. In front of the stands sat Sir Pertab Singh, Regent of Jodhpur and grand old polo player. He is I believe 78 years old now and sits on his horse still beautifully. And all India knows that the Jodhpur team is the apple of his eye, his darling and his pride, and he had coaxed it and nursed it for this fight. Through all this game he sat immovable, not a muscle not an eyelid nor a finger moving. Not even in that last demoniac minute when Jodhpur scored its sixth goal and won. He was a figure carved out of wood. Then as the horn sounded people from all sides broke, cheering and tumultuous, to congratulate him, the Prince [of Wales] among the first. And as the old man stood up, tears poured down his cheeks. 'Now I can die happy!' he exclaimed at last."

At the end of his polo career, recounts Watson, a special tribute was paid to Hanut Singh by the polo correspondent of the *Times*, himself an international player of some renown.

It was always from Number Three that Hanut organized his teams, seldom hitting goals himself, but, with that unforgettable cut-out shot from the sidelines, placing the ball twenty yards in front of the goal for his Number One to tap through. . . . Hanut thinks deeply about all aspects of polo and no one knows more about how to school and produce ponies and players. I think his finest achievement in later life was to win the Cowdray Park Gold Cup for Eric Moller's Jersey Lilies in 1964 and 1965. Hanut selected three unknown young players and collected and supervised the ponies. He was himself then rated at 4 goals, but his brain-power was still equal to his 9-goal handicap, and his meticulous management of the ponies was based on many years of experience. For he was quite the best judge of potential polo ponies of his generation. . . . You never saw Hanut having to put pressure on the reins—a delicate touch and the pony responded. Likewise he could suit ponies to players. . . .

He represents all that is best in the old Rajput aristocracy, which taught the British the way to play polo.

It is significant that Hanut Singh's greatest moments occurred not only at the twilight of Indian polo but at the ages of sixty-four and sixty-five respectively, after the game in that country had long since dried up and was almost exclusively the province of the military. By then polo clubs were located only in major Indian cities like Calcutta and Delhi. It is difficult to speak of contemporary Indian polo, because there is so little of it.

Rao Rajah Hanut Singh was the last of a glorious line of Indian players who stretched backward in time to the very origins of polo. What I admire about him is the thought he gave to the game, and how, two years in a row, he was able to outwit the best that England could offer.

"Once when he was playing holiday polo at a French resort behind a Number One who needed a bit of Dutch courage, Hanut dosed him with brandy and they won the match. Afterwards the Number One said: 'I saw two polo sticks, two polo balls, four ears on my pony and two Hanuts!'" Rao Rajah Hanut Singh may be forgiven if on this occasion he allowed with justifiable pride that there was only one Hanut Singh.

IT WAS BETTER to leave all that history and walk a few hundred yards to a Cowdray Park field in the late misty afternoon and see a game in progress, as if polo were a pickup sport like school-yard basketball. There is always a game, always the chance to see some terrific English or American players.

The best fun was my being accompanied by Colonel Harper, who was a resource of information about polo, had played it around the world, anticipated fouls seconds before they happened, had a discerning eye for

Colonel A. W. Harper rides off Hanut Singh
at Cowdray Park.

good players, especially young Americans like Mike Azzaro, who were getting their chance on an international stage.

A vigorous man in his late seventies, Colonel Harper kept a marvelous reserve and modesty. I once asked him how he had won England's second highest medal for valor, in Malaya during World War II. He made it sound routine, as if he'd been in the neighborhood one day when medals were handed out. He would much rather talk about polo in India, or that tiger he'd bagged in '38.

On any afternoon there was a chance to see a good game. Paul Withers, who ran Cowdray Park's polo operations, might be playing his usual defensive position, hitting bullet forehands and backhands, taking all his team's penalty shots. His wife, Sheldon Withers, would be on the sidelines to make mental notes of the game for discussion afterward with Paul. She knew the intricacies and idiosyncracies of every horse and player on the field. Withers, an excellent seven-goaler, was one of the first English professionals and had played on the English national team.

Sometimes the action spread beyond the field and swirled around parked cars. Sometimes the game came right to me, right in my eyes, with shaking sweat and turf tremble and concentration of players, so strong that I could almost touch it as the horses brushed by the rows of chrome.

At Cowdray Park all those royals and Range Rovers and sneaker manufacturers and champagne companies seemed mercifully far away. One just had the game and the green parkland and that was enough.

At other English polo venues money was everywhere; high-cost Americans were everywhere. A young marquess, a member of the royal family, nursed a pint at the cramped bar of the Guards Polo Club in

The Cowdray Park Gold Cup, 1969.
The Windsor team, from left to right: Umpire
Juan José Diaz Alberdi, Paul Withers,
Prince Philip, the Marquis of Waterford,
and Lord Patrick Beresford

Windsor Park, talking to a couple of English players. The marquess was a pleasant, unaffected young man in his late twenties: fair skin, handsome open face, friendly blue eyes. A good polo player.

The marquess had made a bet that morning with a couple of American patrons. It had to do with whether one English team, led by a Chilean, could defeat another English team, led by a Mexican.

"How much?" the Americans had said to the marquess.

"A hundred quid," replied the marquess. He didn't say it just like that, in the light spirit of the thing. He had to think a second.

The marquess stood in the clubhouse and asked the barflies, "Did I do the right thing? They're both multimillionaires, you know. Maybe a hundred quid wasn't enough."

The marquess's helicopter stood parked outside, ready to whisk him to London. But he thought that he had made a money gaffe.

Nothing was to be said, finally, and the marquess shrugged and went back to talking with his friends about horses and courses.

THERE IS ONE other thing about England, and it happened on a day when past and present collided for me, a gray-soaked afternoon at Windsor Park, where I had a brief interview with Geoffrey Kent, patron of the Windsor Park team, who told me how polo's lessons of teamwork and leadership helped him in business.

The rest of the Windsor Park team arrived, and I was introduced to a young American seven-goaler named Bobby Barry. He was a big-boned, high-level player in his late twenties. Suddenly the patron, the heavy royalty on hand, the game itself, interested me not at all.

"Are you the son of Roy Barry?" I asked the young man. He nodded.

Somewhere behind me Prince Charles pulled up in his sports car. I dimly perceived a rush of glances in his direction. The prince's team-mates, including the young Texan, had been waiting for him.

"I saw your father play in Argentina in 1966," I said. "Against Juan Carlos Harriott's team."

Bobby Barry nodded again, proffered a friendly grin. Texans are extremely polite. "Yeah, I heard he played down there." Argentina was a vagueness to him; he had been a child in 1966.

"He was great."

The young man looked pleased, and I was glad to get out that least bit. I had more to say, wondered if father and son had ever spoken of the complex journeys of that one game two decades ago. How Roy Barry had leaned out of the saddle like a steer wrestler, fought the best polo team in the world to a standstill.

The Americans had lost in 1966. Roy Barry missed crucial penalty shots. In the end, to the extent it existed for anyone in memory, the game had been just another victory racked up by the Argentineans a long time ago.

I particularly recall the callow anger that I reserved for the nerve-shaken Barry, who had blown those penalties. It looked so easy. The gaping goal, the merest tap-in, the game ours—that is, the United States.

It was not easy, of course. The young Texan had been exhausted. Against the Argentineans it had been necessary to play a mistake-free defensive game while almost always being on the attack. This style of play led to vast gaps in the field that the Argentineans plunged through at will.

Nothing is more devastating to an opponent than teamwork at a high level. Pass, pass, pass, pass—score. Then the Americans would roar up-field like Saracens to get the goal back.

Abruptly, the action stopped.

That afternoon in 1966 Roy Barry rode alone into a cauldron of Argentinean polo fans—fifteen thousand of them and millions more watching on television. A reign of quietness, and the silence unnerved him. He made impossible goals, weird-angled shots at full gallop as if he were about to jump off his horse, scooping the ball and his body up from inches off the ground. He had been doing it all day; he had kept the U.S. team in the game.

Don Meredith, the former quarterback of the Dallas Cowboys, once defined "pressure" as the cold rush of shit to the heart.

I wanted to get inside the game with Bobby Barry, tell him about his father. I would omit those missed penalty shots. But Bobby had the upcoming match on his mind and the social paraphernalia that went with it. The Prince of Wales had ridden out onto the field. One forgets, traveling among the young, that not everyone is held by memories.

Perhaps it has no relevance, but as I stood in the saddling area after the game and watched horses being loaded into their vans, saw first the Duchess of York and then the Prince of Wales leave the club, just standing there idly as it began to rain . . . all I could think of—last meditations upon the day—were lines from D. H. Lawrence's poem "The Snake."

In the poem Lawrence, the greatest nature writer in English, steps onto his veranda in Italy, encounters a large black snake, becomes frightened, throws a stick at it. Instantly the snake, which has been basking innocently in the sun, retreats into a hole.

In the poem Lawrence berates himself for his human fear and how it abruptly supplants his hunger to observe a natural phenomenon. He laments the distance between himself, his weaknesses of guilt and fear, and this creature. The poem is elegiac and suffused with regret. The be-

Carlos Gracida

ginning of the last stanza is a glory: "I missed my chance with one of the lords/Of life."

Thinking of snakes in what at that moment was the most glitz-ridden environment imaginable. It was as if a bridge had been created for me to cross into another era, if I could but make the connection.

I stood in the rain at Windsor Park, in that world of hard celebrity, snakes, and love.

THE OUTSTANDING polo player in England that summer of 1988 was a young ten-goal Mexican named Carlos Gracida. I had already seen him several times in Argentina and the States, and in England I watched him every chance I could. His game was on a plane different than anyone else's.

One afternoon something extraordinary happened. Gracida was playing for his English team, called Tremontana, against one of the better English fours. Up to that point, the match was undistinguished. Gracida played well, blending in, and the score was close. Because he was a big star, he tended to get converged upon.

He took the ball at the side of his own goal and was caught in traffic. Some of it was caused by his teammates, who hung back waiting to see what he would do. There is a tendency in mediocre polo to let the star do the work.

He could have slammed the ball upfield, but an opposition player might have reached it first and stroked it through an open goal.

Gracida kept the ball on his mallet in a mass of players, making forays and thrusts and parries as he searched for an opening. The entire field looked like someone's rolling, unoccupied lawn, as players clotted in a little area around him.

Opponents lunged for the ball; horses swirled and kicked up turf. Gracida made tiny, intricate maneuvers of such sureness and delicacy that he might as easily have been rolling the ball away from outstretched mallet heads by hand. Now thrusting out the ball, now drawing it back onto his mallet in stern rebuke, now turning his horse to block an opponent, now pushing and pulling and curling the ball around a threatening mallet. Though he was hopelessly trapped, he appeared to be saying to his enemies, Now I've got you just where I want you.

He never looked directly at the ball; rather, he searched for a passage between horses where he could slip through and get into open field. He seemed to have all day to meditate upon the aggressions of his opponents, welcoming them into his finespun web.

He did not forget his role as field general. All during this intricate maneuvering he gave orders to his teammates, which I could hear clearly because the action took place near the grandstand. But they looked mesmerized by his brilliant actions of mallet and ball and stayed in place. The other team yelled, too, swearing at the prolongation of this episode now that they had him trapped.

His long mallet seemed an extension of his hand.

Carlos Gracida's thirty seconds with the ball on his mallet, playing hide-and-seek with it for a breathtaking time, was a remarkable performance. Horses bumped him; mallets flailed; he had himself and his horse to coordinate mathematically while avoiding seven others.

Everything he did required distinguished concentration and dramatic poise. He was serenity in the storm, confident that daylight would break and he would eventually get out of there and back to safety.

I believe that if a patch of daylight had not opened up, his opponents would never have taken the ball from him unless they fouled him. He would have continued to make his dainty nudges, his exquisite drawings-back, his miniaturist strokes, and with his horse would have constructed a series of fortresses against attack.

Carlos Gracida was four feet above the ball at all times. He didn't carry it under his arm; he didn't dribble it from palm to hard court like a basketball; he didn't push it like a hockey puck along level ice. No artificial turf made the bounces smoother. This was real churned-up grass, and the ball took funny bounces, and he kept it glued to a mallet head six inches long and two inches high. It was something very hard to accomplish—impossible to do for so many seconds. He had total confidence in himself and made it seem inconceivable that he would lose control of the ball. Sooner or later he would end his search and get out of there.

Eventually, an opponent got too close, and a shard of light broke open. Gracida spurred his horse and fled down a tiny avenue, urging the ball in front of him. He galloped far enough away to force the teams to spread out, and then he made his pass.

The way he kept time all to himself and sucked in the air of the stadium.

Peter Orthwein

Chapter Six

THAT SUMMER of 1988 I watched Americans and the best Argentineans playing outside Greenwich, Connecticut. The polo fields there were part of an expensive multiacre compound featuring houses owned by the likes of Ivan Lendl and the president of the World Wrestling Federation. Hulk Hogan had been spotted on the grounds. The cost to buy a ten-to-twenty-eight-acre property on the compound was $1.8 to $2.2 million.

The driving force in U.S. high-goal polo for the last few years—whether in Connecticut, Saratoga Springs, or Palm Beach—has been a man named Peter Brant. To describe him as controversial is the least of it; he is not widely liked in polo circles. A run-in with the Internal Revenue Service in 1990 over $2.5 million resulted in a ninety-day prison sentence.

Brant has been described as a Gatsby-like figure, but nothing is romantic about him, and no green light flickers at the end of the dock. Though he does not ride well, he compensates with great horses and terrific hand-to-eye coordination. As a result, he has risen to seven goals, making him the highest ranked amateur player in the United States.

His team won everything that summer in Greenwich—one of many polo leagues spread around the country—but in the final contest of the season his opponents came from behind and tied the score as time ran out. The game should have gone into sudden-death overtime; the fans expected it, the public-address announcer announced it, but Brant decided to end it as a tie. After all, it was his field. I don't think he wanted to risk going into sudden death, where anything might happen to mar his undefeated season. He moved among his opponents, saying, as if he took the game casually, as if it were just a sport to him and he hadn't invested millions of dollars in it to outfit himself with the best players and horses, "What do you say we call it a day?"

In the major polo finals held every spring in Palm Beach, Brant's team, White Birch, had won the tournament for several consecutive years. That was expected, since his team featured three ten-goal Argentineans. He never was defeated with them and in victory was gracious.

When Brant finally lost a big game, it happened in Palm Beach on a late-April afternoon in 1990. The great Mexican, Carlos Gracida, scored the winning goal in the last seconds to beat Brant's team.

After threatening rain all afternoon, the Florida skies opened during the trophy presentation ceremonies. Brant looked up and said, "I don't think God meant for that team to win."

ONE GREENWICH four was sponsored by a phone company. The sponsor, a nonplayer, smoked long cigars. He had two sons who competed for the phone club. They too smoked cigars. For some reason they were given to making exclamations in French.

On a Tuesday afternoon, during a practice game, the field umpire made a questionable call on a play. The call could have gone either way, but this was practice, and perhaps fifteen people were watching from the clubhouse veranda. It was not a big deal.

The sons, wreathed in cigar smoke, standing among the spectators, cupped their hands and yelled at the umpire across the field, where he rode around waiting for the next period to begin.

The umpire that day happened to be the best active player in the world, Gonzalo Pieres. He was taking a break from his more arduous chores as leader of Peter Brant's White Birch team to umpire this game.

Gonzalo Pieres is my favorite polo player.

The sons yelled at him that he had missed the call. No foul had taken place. What was he, blind?

He took the razzing in stride, so to speak.

The sons paced around the veranda for a couple of minutes, creating a sideshow, trying to whip up support for their cause. Then they began to shout at the umpire again, until the next period mercifully began. The father looked on approvingly, chewing on his cigar.

The sons were not more than eighteen or nineteen years old. Much can be explained away.

Still . . .

I thought about sportsmanship, and one incident kept coming to mind. Forty years ago and more, an American polo team journeyed down to Buenos Aires to play against the Argentineans. The Americans hadn't been any good at polo since before World War II. It was not expected they would do well, and they didn't.

The Argentineans had the best horses and players. They could assemble more than eight hundred horses to select from; the Americans had about twenty-five, shipped down from the United States. Often the Americans purchased horses while in Argentina. Often that was the point of making the long trip.

On the second day of their visit, the Americans played a practice game against the best Argentineans. More to get acquainted than anything else, a social match. The game was held on one of the outlying polo fields at Palermo Stadium. Palermo is the center of the sport; the best polo has been played there for more than half a century.

In the first period a penalty was called against an Argentinean. An American player got ready to hit the penalty shot, with the ball placed sixty yards from the goal.

The American cantered up to the ball to stroke the shot, thought better of it, and cantered back to have another go. This is perfectly legal in polo. Sometimes the shot just doesn't feel right, particularly in a sport in which two athletes need to be coordinated—horse and rider. Perhaps the American was nervous; perhaps he was riding a strange horse. Anyway, he did what he did. And that was fine.

When the American didn't take the first shot, an Argentinean ten-goaler waited impatiently on his horse near the goal.

The Argentinean player muttered under his breath, *"Puta."*

Puta means "whore," but the Argentinean meant it more as "God-dammit." The Argentineans are great sportsmen and individualists. The player was just expressing mild, momentary annoyance that the penalty shot had been delayed. Perhaps he was annoyed because he had caused the penalty. He did not expect to be overheard.

He was banned from polo for a year. He was not allowed to stick around for the penalty shot or finish out the period. The umpire who heard the utterance ordered him off the field. The Argentineans immediately brought in a substitute. That was that.

I've thought about the harmless *"puta"* and the umpire's no-nonsense ejection. At first I didn't believe the story. Nobody gets hooked for muttering; the punishment seems almost medieval. But in the context of polo it was entirely justifiable and, if anything, too lenient. Lower the standards a fraction, yell at umpires as in Yankee Stadium, allow a glimmer of darkness for chaos to slip through, and sooner or later the highest price will be paid in a fall or collision. Polo is very formal in this sense.

PETER ORTHWEIN is a patron and a good polo player. He runs his own company, Thor Industries, which makes Airstream trailers. An heir to the Anheuser-Busch brewery fortune, Orthwein is an unassuming man who loves polo. He was a fine player at Cornell, hits a tremendous shot, rides well, carries a five-goal handicap. Orthwein holds his own with the professionals whom he hires.

He takes his polo seriously. His team that summer of 1988 consisted of himself; an American professional named Adam Snow; and Alfonso Pieres, a ten-goaler who had won many Argentinean national championships. A fourth man, whom I thought of as the player to be named later, was seldom a factor in the game and often seemed to be competing on a different field.

Occasionally Adam Snow had other polo commitments. Then Orthwein would take the field with Alfonso Pieres and two poor players. The opposing team often had the same problem. Orthwein frequently participated in matches where the opposition had three good men to his two, or four to his three.

After a match it was not necessary to say much to Orthwein except, "Three against two." He would smile wearily. When he or Alfonso Pieres hit a great shot, no teammate rode out front to take the pass. The ball landed softly on an expanse of empty field.

Or the reverse happened: the opposing four broke through the Orthwein-Pieres defenses. Since the Orthwein team lacked a decent defensive player (that being traditionally the province of the woeful) again this swath of field was exposed and an easy goal created for the opposition.

The defensive player often had trouble enough controlling his horse. It would have been asking a great deal of him actually to make a play.

There was too much empty field, too many players who did not perform as a cohesive unit. Some looked as if they had been separated from the ebb and flow of the game for undefined reasons. Some looked like dreamers—quixotic, literary—wandering around meditatively on horseback.

After the game Orthwein would shake his head and walk away. Three against two, two against one, four against three—it made no difference; this wasn't why he had taken up the game. What you look for in anyone is love and the human response to violations of love.

Alfonso Pieres loved the game, too, not just because it had taken him from humble origins in Argentina to heights of glamour. Sometimes his love led to frustrations. He was like a man who had spent his life racing Formula 1 cars at 230 miles per hour and now was reduced to driving Buicks.

When Pieres became frustrated he was a sight. He never got angry with the Americans—a wise career move. Orthwein sometimes had to step in and deal harshly with Pieres, telling him to stop yelling and get on with the game. Only then did Alfonso calm down. This was more than just a matter of the owner's having the last word; the two men were confreres.

After a particularly sloppy play, Pieres deflected his anger against American ineptitude by attacking in vile language an opposing Argentinean professional for allegedly committing a monstrous foul. I was never entirely sure that Pieres's counterpart had indeed committed the foul in question, but Alfonso yelled at him in Spanish. Fortunately in Spanish, because the nicest thing he had to say at the top of his lungs was, "Shit comes out of your mother's ass." Sportsmanship really took a pounding.

This was a set piece of every game: Alfonso's aria. His counterpart always took the tantrums in stride. These great poloists had been playing together or against each other for a long time. They lapped up the money during the American summer and went south for the Argentinean summer, when they played serious polo.

Alfonso Pieres is a slightly built, good-looking, blond man with quick movements, a quick smile, and the bandy walk of a man who has spent his life on horseback.

Polo players come in all shapes and sizes, from three-hundred-pound Texas beef boys to men the size of jockeys. Size is not talent, but boxing and polo share one maxim: The bigger they are, the harder they fall. American players tend to be the biggest. Too many championships have been lost because heavyweight stars fell off their horses and departed by ambulance.

Alfonso Pieres is the quickest to the ball in all of polo. He has a trigonometrist's ability to cut through traffic by the shortest route possible to make his shot. This has less to do with his horse's speed—though that is important, too—than with a talent for seeing a play develop and getting to the center of the action in a few strides.

Alfonso has this artistic temperament.

THE WIVES of the Argentinean players formed an enclave in Greenwich during that summer of 1988. They sat around discussing shopping expeditions. Born to makeup, high heels, and bangled dresses, they had their priorities.

Alfonso Pieres at left and Alberto Heguy
in white, 1987

I stood near the horses opposite the grandstand on the main field, making notes during a Sunday match. The floating group of Argentinean wives perched under a maple tree nearby. Their children played around them, scampering up and down a grassy bank. Several boys held sawed-off polo mallets.

In the closing seconds of the game, with the score tied, a fabulous play transpired. A serious foul was committed, and a player rode out to hit a forty-five-yard penalty shot at an unguarded goal. This shot is equivalent to kicking a point after touchdown in football or a gimme putt in golf. Good polo players—and the best one on the team takes the penalty shot—rarely miss from forty-five yards.

The certain goal would break the tie and end the game. Not enough time remained on the clock for the other side to get downfield and score. To make matters worse, it was illegal for an opposing player to move inside the goalposts until after the shot was hit.

At the precise moment that mallet struck ball, a player at the edge of my vision swept across the goal in a blue blur with mallet raised. He did not just deflect the ball—feat enough—but swung at it and slammed it out-of-bounds fifty yards in front of him. He might as well have been the player taking the penalty shot for all the accuracy and leisure he put into his dazzling interception.

The penalty shot as hit must have been traveling at one hundred miles per hour, a dot of white in the landscape rising to the height of a horse's shoulder. Then at the goal line it was snatched in midair from certain victory.

The interception happened so quickly, was so impossibly accomplished, that I awaited thunderous applause from the crowd. But the great shot was over before it could be absorbed and relished. By the time one might have applauded, the players were straggling back to midfield for the toss-in.

All I could think of in the moments after the shot was to get the player's name. Since he had been traveling from left to right, I couldn't see his number. I turned to the Argentinean wives and asked eagerly, "Who was that?" To a wife, they stared at me blankly. One of them, a pencil-thin woman with black hair and a deep tan, got up slowly, brushed her sundress, climbed the grassy bank, and surveyed the field as a general might survey a trench battle far, far away through binoculars.

"*Yo no se,*" she said, and shook her head. I don't know. Not just that she didn't know who had made the interception; she didn't know who was playing. Time began for her when her husband in his dirty uniform came to fetch her and the kids and packed them into their rented Taurus.

After a minute she shrugged, turned, and went back to the arrayed group of wives.

I DECIDED that fitness might be an important angle I could pursue for this book. I would learn how fitness or the lack of it affected the quality of play.

I went to have a talk with The Man. In polo, The Man is Gonzalo Pieres, who was the premier player in the world in the 1980s. He is the brother of Alfonso Pieres, the Orthwein team's star.

Gonzalo and Alfonso Pieres play on the same teams so often that they frequently come as a boxed set. They have won most matches, including several Argentinean national championships, which is the standard of measure. Gonzalo was the anchor of an Argentinean team called La Espadaña, which has since disbanded. That team consisted of:

Gonzalo Pieres, 1991

Polo: The Emperor of Games

1. Carlos Gracida (10 goals)
2. Alfonso Pieres (10 goals)
3. Gonzalo Pieres (10 goals)
4. Ernesto Trotz (10 goals)

It was one of the great polo fours in history.

Players out to earn their spurs—young talents from South America and polo enclaves in the United States, Chileans, and Mexicans—measure themselves against The Man. They know a thing or two but learn quickly that they don't know enough. Gonzalo is getting older, and they think it is time for him to slip. It would be dramatic to say that Gonzalo deals them a stern cuffing for their presumption. But his style is not about cuffings.

One sunny afternoon in Connecticut, a round-robin practice game had been going on, but for some reason The Man wasn't playing that day.

He stood by the field wearing faded jeans and a yellow sports shirt.

I began explaining to him in elaborate detail how the patrons—the so-called amateurs—of polo trained. It was a lengthy preamble to a simple question.

He listened patiently to my descriptions of various fitness regimens. The pages of my notebook flapped. I misread bafflement for contempt on his face. Once before, in Argentina a few days prior to La Espadaña's final against a tough opponent, I had attempted to ask Gonzalo Pieres a question—Did he expect a fast game?—and he had looked at me steadily without answering, then turned away. Someone once described baseball star Mickey Mantle's stare as resembling the nictitating membrane in the eye of a bird. Gonzalo's had been like that.

Concluding my preamble, I hoped Gonzalo would give me at least five pages of good stuff. Surely he must retreat to a spa in the Cayman Islands and put himself in the hands of professional fitness-aerobics people, with the dedication and heart of a unique modern athlete. This would mitigate somewhat polo's image with most people—or "mostpeople," as e. e. cummings put it—as strictly for the rich.

"I never exercise," Gonzalo said. "I can't run ten feet."

A half smile flitted across my face. Surely he jested.

He coughed. "See that car?" Gonzalo pointed to a blue Maserati Biturbo parked a few feet from where we stood. "I couldn't run over there."

He didn't need to bullshit anyone. Maybe he couldn't run ten feet, but his horse did the speed work. He wanted me to know that.

What impressed me about him were his evenhandedness, competitive disinterest, and level temperament; his awareness that he would win most of the time, but not every time. He never chipped in sly digs about people. Losing did not eat away at him, the way I think it did with patrons who couldn't play one-tenth as well.

His calm generosity toward his opponents. His detachment. He viewed polo from an elevated position, as a kind of player emeritus.

I asked him about other Argentinean players. Clinically, he described their strengths and weaknesses. He told me that when he was younger, he got so wired on the morning of a big match that he would play in a practice game just to work off nervous energy.

Young days were gone. Gonzalo Pieres was in his midthirties.

He didn't come at me in sections, pushing his ego, describing the great difficulties incurred during his career. He had ascended from nowhere; he wasn't an aristocrat in this most aristocratic of sports; he had risen on skill alone.

Life was now good to him. In Argentina he had built his redbrick dream house, which overlooked his own personal polo field, in a place called Pilarchico. I had seen the house while visiting another player. I mentioned to Gonzalo that it must be nice having his own polo field.

"Yes," he said with a broad smile. By nature he was not a smiler. "It has been a dream." Normally a reserved, almost taciturn man, for a moment he looked truly happy on that pleasant afternoon. His young son, Gonzalito, played around us on the grass with a miniature polo mallet.

Gonzalo Pieres is of medium height with a slim build, though slightly heavier than his brother, the mercurial Alfonso. He has thinning blond hair, graying slightly, and a mustache. He looks average in the way that a professional golfer looks average.

We discussed his brother and teammate. Gonzalo said that Alfonso was much quicker to the ball than he. His voice trailed off a bit, and I sensed that he thought that while Alfonso was quicker to the ball, Gonzalo might know a shade more of what to do when he got to it.

Evenhanded, neutral: Gonzalo might have been talking about himself in the third person.

If people wish to see how the game should be played, they should go see Gonzalo Pieres on a July Sunday in Greenwich, or an April Sunday in Palm Beach, or an August Sunday afternoon in Saratoga Springs.

Two months after our talks, he defined why he is The Man. On a September day in Greenwich the Argentineans played the Americans in a game called the Championship of the Americas. The Argentineans consisted of four ten-goalers: three players from La Espadaña plus a tengoaler named Christian Laprida substituting for Carlos Gracida, who was under contract to play in France for Guy Wildenstein, a wealthy art dealer. The Argentineans lost nothing by having Laprida on their team.

The American team consisted of:

Frank Milburn

1. Mike Azzaro (8 goals)
2. Tommy Waymann (8 goals)
3. Owen Rinehart (9 goals)
4. Dale Smiklas (8 goals)

Mike Azzaro, still in his twenties, may be the next great American player. (He was raised to nine goals in 1989.) However, on this day he suffered cold rushes and overran or topped balls.

Tommy Waymann, a Texan, had once been the only American with a ten-goal handicap. He was past his prime and not a factor in the game.

Owen Rinehart, a Virginian, was a good classical polo player but perhaps overvalued at nine goals. He lacked bumptiousness, an American characteristic. He played as if he were the Second Coming of Juan Carlos Harriott: distant, lordly. (In 1992 Rinehart was raised to ten goals.)

Dale Smiklas was a solid defensive player without much flair.

The Argentineans got several goals ahead and promptly, inexplicably, seemed to fall asleep in their saddles on that sunny afternoon, with a crowd of about five thousand on hand. The Americans crept back into the game, and a wonderful play occurred.

The ball sat next to the sideboards, and suddenly I felt a gathering heaviness of concentration, like the threatening placidity before a major storm.

Gonzalo Pieres attacked the ball at full gallop, with a heightened poise at the farthest edge of equilibrium. He was so tilted that I thought he and the horse might go down. Every fiber of muscle and mallet was stretched to the limit.

At first I figured he had mis-hit the ball, but in fact he made something like a fade shot in golf, sphere curving gently and deposited as if with loving care, fragilely, a few strides in front of an onrushing Christian Laprida, riding one hundred yards upfield. Laprida could have knocked the ball through the goal easily from thirty yards out, but he shepherded it through at an easy canter.

What broke the Americans was Gonzalo's coolness, as if to declare, I can do this all day. Make fabulous shots from dangerous angles. If you raise your game, he seemed to tell the Americans, I will raise mine a level higher.

The rest of the match was a mess, but afterward, during the trophy-presentation ceremonies, all the Americans I talked to insisted it had been an excellent contest.

I spoke to the umpire, a fine seven-goal Argentinean who played on the New Jersey and upstate New York polo circuit, from Mahwah to Millbrook to Gilbertsville. I liked him a lot, not least because after winning one match he gave me his prize—ten coffee mugs with polo scenes painted on them. Perhaps in the course of his summer tournaments he had received many coffee mugs.

The umpire shrugged. "The Argentineans should have won by twenty goals." Something in his shrug spoke of contempt for the game's sloppiness—as if to say, If you Yanks are going to play at championship level, show up with more than overeager or over-the-hill players. Bring a little more to the party next time.

When I asked Gonzalo Pieres about the match, he didn't bat an eye, standing in his light-blue jersey and dirt-streaked riding breeches, lacking the imposition of strength that he possessed when aboard a horse. "The Americans played very well," he said. "They caught us by surprise. It was all we could do to stay in the game."

"It was all you could do to stay awake," I said.

Gonzalo Pieres gave a tight smile and shrugged. He was heading back to Buenos Aires that night, to begin the Argentinean season. His wife stood behind him, holding the gaudy gold trophy her husband had just won. Not exactly holding it, but dragging it a bit as she organized her children for the trip home. Dangling the trophy from her hand, so it brushed along the ground. Her husband had won a thousand matches; this was one more.

"Give me a call when you get to BA," Gonzalo said to me with a wave, just before being engulfed by more well-wishers. Yes, it was a tough game, and we were lucky to pull it out.... This is the best American team I've seen in a long time....

On that high, false note, the American polo season ended.

Marcos Heguy at left, 1991

Chapter Seven

ARGENTINA IS a tragic country, inspiring theatrics. In Greek tragedy the sin of smugness, not hubris, brings down the hero.

Argentina is a morose country. It has melancholy memories and depressing expectations. The Colombian novelist Gabriel García Márquez wrote acidly of "the little Argentine in all of us."

One November afternoon, just before my wife (who is Argentinean) and I took our seats at Palermo Stadium for a championship match, a spectator spotted me for an American and said, "Polo is the only thing we Argentineans do well."

It was a sad remark, totally inaccurate. Argentina raises the finest beef. Its soccer teams, especially when Diego Maradona was playing, are among the best in the world. Argentina won the World Cup in 1986. They have excellent doctors, scientists, engineers, businessmen, artists.

They have Borges and Puig. Juan Fangio. Gato Barbieri. In the Teatro Colón they have an acoustical wonder. They have more climates than any country in the world, from jungle to glacier to desert. They have Gabriela Sabatini. They have the world's most complex and resonant dance—tango.

·   ·   ·

A MOVIE called *The Official Story,* an Academy Award winner for best foreign film, captures Argentina. Complicities and ignoble aspirations are spread out before the viewer like that famous patient etherized.

Throughout the film, a little girl named Gaby, whose parents were murdered by death squads and who afterward was adopted illegally by a bourgeois couple, sings a nursery rhyme that gathers poignancy. The rhyme begins: "In the land of I-don't-remember. . . ." When I think about Argentina, that refrain is somewhere in my mind.

Almost all bourgeois and upper-class Argentineans hated the film.

ONCE IN Buenos Aires I sat with a group of polo aficionados during a national championship. My soul and body were with an underdog team of young riders. I overrooted, situated there among the creamery butter of Buenos Aires society. They were a bunch of mild applauders at best.

I must have figured a hockey game had broken out. I still wince to think of it. I wolfed down whatever the food vendors tossed my way, rocked in my seat, loud-hailed good shots, groaned at bad ones, made clenched fists of victory when "we" scored a goal. I became nervous during an important penalty shot, and in the tension-riddled final period, I nearly became sick.

My youthful band lost by one goal. Tremendous game. Every player had been riding since he was in diapers. The teams galloped up and down the field in a prolonged series of brilliant cavalry charges.

A dignified old man wearing an immaculate, white linen suit leaned over to me. I recognized him as a great Argentinean poloist of the 1930s. With his perfect British accent, he said, "I say, you certainly put a lot of enthusiasm into the game."

Less a tone of reprimand than of amazement, as if I'd wandered into this temple of polo from a soccer riot.

All the fans in the opposite grandstand—the Palermo Stadium holds about fifteen thousand people—were in the same ebullient spirit as I, waving flags and shouting *Arriba!* at their favorites. They sat in the cheap seats, baking in the heavy afternoon sun, and their joy led me astray. I assumed that everyone got into the game. I was obviously sitting in the wrong section.

Alfonso Pieres captained the team that defeated my young riders on that Sunday in Buenos Aires. The next year fabled La Espadaña included Alfonso and Gonzalo Pieres, Carlos Gracida, and Ernesto Trotz— ten-goalers all.

The only way to beat La Espadaña was by guile, speed, luck, guerrilla insurgency, and something that my young riders—who formed a team called Indios—had perfected. This was the continual shifting of position so that the same front was never shown.

La Espadaña was the closest I have ever seen in sports to Jaws, the eating-machine shark of the movies.

Sometimes Indios got Jaws; sometimes Jaws got them. They had to risk their necks all afternoon just to keep Espadaña at bay. When I say risk their necks, I'm being literal. This was polo at its highest level. Matches between these two teams, Indios and La Espadaña, were sometimes death defying, and in my opinion became the most savage battles in the history of modern sports.

In Argentina I witnessed a scene involving Gonzalito Pieres, the nine-year-old son of Gonzalo Pieres. It took place at the polo fields in Pilarchico, a town near Buenos Aires where the Pieres brothers and several top players have their houses.

At the close of afternoon, after a practice game involving several Brazilians who had come to buy horses, the lovely scene occurred. It has stayed in my mind, its gentleness after mallet clashes.

Into a sweet silence appeared Gonzalito Pieres. He rode a chestnut pony and held a regulation mallet. In his small hands the mallet resembled a circus prop designed for a man on stilts. Gonzalito jounced along the fringes of the polo field, his short legs dangling, with the stirrups raised up nearly to a jockey's position.

As Gonzalito rode around, there appeared behind him Carlos Gracida, the ten-goal Mexican who played number 1 for La Espadaña, riding a black polo horse. On this afternoon the dark-haired young Gracida wore khakis and a blue windbreaker. He was checking out a horse, getting in some solitary practice.

This was a Thursday. On the following Sunday the finals of the 1988 Argentinean national championships—polo's Super Bowl—would take place at Palermo Stadium. La Espadaña was seeking to avenge a shocking defeat suffered the previous year at the hands of Indios.

Gonzalito had a ball and a mallet, but couldn't get any momentum going because he kept missing the ball. Every few yards he had to stop, turn his pony, and go back to get it. All of this was unwieldy for a nine-year-old—turning his horse, trotting back, lifting the mallet, taking a short shot.

Then Carlos Gracida rode onto the field aboard his black horse, and the two of them—polo star and polo star's son—got into a rhythm. When Gonzalito missed the ball, Gracida hit it back up to him, placing it unerringly on Gonzalito's mallet with a soft lofted shot dropped just slightly ahead of the tiny scythe of Gonzalito's mallet stroke.

Gonzalito missed a few times, but Gracida kept the game going. Time after time he made the same unerring shot for Gonzalito, all the while maintaining a steady canter and checking the gait and speed and reflexes of his own horse for the upcoming championship.

What impressed me was Carlos Gracida's seriousness. He might just as well have been practicing with Gonzalito's father. Together they could have been working out intricate championship strategy; a give-and-go, perhaps; a new wrinkle for Espadaña to use against the champion Indios.

Gonzalito became happier and more secure as he got into his own timing and knew that the ball would be passed up to him accurately, so he wouldn't have to waste a precious minute turning his thick pony and going back for the ball. The effect on him was mesmeric, the action conducted in happy silence, made memorable after an afternoon of shouts from the Brazilians.

After a couple of laps around the field, they broke off, and the tiny moment ended without a word. Gonzalito rode back to the stables, and Carlos took more professional turns. That was fun to watch, too, because he was a splendid rider. Sometimes he put his horse into bursts of speed, like overdrive, and then stopped it again abruptly. These bursts seemed very important to him—not long gallops, but dashes of ten or fifteen yards. From zero to thirty-five miles per hour in as short a time as possible, that's what he wanted the horse for: a few bursts when spurred.

A professional polo player like Carlos Gracida travels the world and rides the horses that he is given, makes do. It would be better, though horrendously expensive, if he could use his own horses, as was often done in the past. They are as important to a polo player as golf clubs are to a professional linksman. A golfer is not handed a club bag before a major tournament and told, "Play with these." He has spent years with his clubs; they are as comfortable to his hands as tender gloves. The same is true of a tennis player and his racquets.

Often a polo player must adjust in days to strange horses. He never gets the opportunity to know them well. All the horses are fine—great, in fact, the best Argentina can offer—but unless a player knows his mount over time, he can never be certain how it reacts to extremes.

For Carlos Gracida, a horrific moment had come and gone in less time than it takes to snap a finger.

Thirty seconds remained in the 1987 national championships. The score was tied. La Espadaña threatened—Gracida and the Pieres brothers and Ernesto Trotz swarmed the Indios goal. Espadaña knew how to put the boot to the enemy's throat.

The game had been fascinating on a number of counts. It had been extraordinarily fast. It had been a tremendous surprise. It had redefined how polo is played. It had ended abruptly on a goal that will be talked about for as long as the sport is remembered.

Even now, it is known in polo circles simply as The Goal.

La Espadaña had no weaknesses; the team was so much better than its opponents that final scores could be comical. Once, after it had brutalized his team, an excellent player named Gonzalo Tanoira, a former ten-goaler, displaced his anger and became enraged at the field, as if that were the opponent. The hard turf itself; the essence of grass. He stared, kicked, became furious at it.

It made no difference that La Espadaña had played on the same field. A fine person otherwise, Tanoira menaced the grass. I thought he was going to dig a hole. Nutty but understandable. Espadaña had done its job when great polo players cursed the ground.

Espadaña's stars did everything in polo as well as it could be done. Their problem, if I can call it that, was that they didn't welcome a fan into the proceedings of their victories or their rare losses. They never won by hook or by crook, never escaped by the skin of their teeth. They never came from behind, because they were always ahead.

They did not convey joy in victory. This wasn't a fault; it was a personality thing with them, as with some great teams. They gave off an aura that victory was owed to them by fiat, and had the arrogance of feeling owed.

Just as people hated the New York Yankees in their prime of Ruth and Gehrig and DiMaggio, there was some of that feeling about La Espadaña. They were not likable. They were not a little guy's team. They were a high roller's team. They were a put-your-money-where-your-mouth-is team. They were who they were; they had achieved a perfect integration of skills. Perfect teamwork, perfect balance.

But La Espadaña could not afford to lose two national championships in a row. A defeat would lower their asking price among the patrons for the great money seasons in the United States, Europe, and England. If they were no longer invincible—if, in fact, that Indios miracle goal had not been a fluke and the loss was repeated—then the patrons would be saying of Indios, I want those guys on my team. Word gets around.

This is how The Goal happened in the Argentinean national championships in 1987. There were thirty seconds left in the game, and the score was tied.

The ball floated beside the goalmouth waiting for a final sword stroke. Gaped, set up for the pulverizing shot from Carlos Gracida or Alfonso Pieres or Gonzalo Pieres or Ernesto Trotz. All of them poised, yet fatally drawn in toward the goal.

The great expanse of field spread out behind them like a spring meadow. Just a fraction of a second there when the ball lay ready for the shot that would have clanked off the scoreboard thirty feet behind the goal; one of those real bullets that puts the exclamation point on a victory.

It was Carlos Gracida's shot. He needed a stride to get to the ball and slam it through the goal. It wasn't his fault. He put his foot on the gas, pedal to the metal . . . and the motor hesitated.

A ghastly moment. Theories abound—the horse was green, unfit for championship play; the horse was tired; the horse was this, and the horse was that. We'll never know.

The fact is, the horse did not respond. It was horrible, the ball and the open goal and being unable to get to it, like running out of gas a yard before the finish line at Indianapolis and feeling the wind rushes of passing cars. Like a nightmare of chasing something and never catching up.

The horse did something that in polo is known as sitting down. It gathered its haunches and sank a bit toward the grass. Carlos Gracida had the shot; he didn't have the horse.

Mistakes are never forgiven at this level of polo. The ball sat in the brief open space in front of the goal. Gracida's moment was gone.

Nobody expected what happened next. Taking his chance for Indios was a brilliant nine-goal player named Marcos Heguy. He was twenty years old. The following year he would be raised to ten goals.

Marcos was the latest in a long line of great polo-playing Heguys. They were a family that, like the Alberdis and Harriotts and Dorignacs, went back a long way in the sport.

There was the man, and in the last period when everyone was tired, Marcos Heguy had the horsepower. He also had the genius of youth or possibly was crazy.

Heguy got to the ball after Gracida's horse sat down. He should have just cleared it safely toward the sideboards. Then the teams could have cuffed around for the remaining seconds, let time run out, and gone into sudden death.

In sudden death I think Espadaña would have adopted a conservative style, set up an impenetrable defense, and waited for a mistake from Indios. Because they were so young and fluid, with such flair for drama, the lads would eventually have made an epic mistake. Like most youthful teams they made the impossible look easy. They also made the easy look impossible.

I don't think Indios wanted to get into sudden death with Espadaña. However, those considerations were probably not running through Marcos Heguy's mind when he reached the ball and took his chance.

First, he committed the one unforgivable sin in any sport played with a fixed goal, whether hockey, soccer, lacrosse, or polo. The immortal textbook of games is clear on this point: *Never carry the ball across your own goalmouth.*

The textbook dictates that a player clear the ball or, if greatly pressed, just knock it out-of-bounds. A player must never leave himself exposed to the interception—or, in this case, the chance that a member of Espadaña might swoop in from Heguy's blind side and through sheer force of momentum press the ball through the goal.

There was practically no time on the clock, a championship on the line. An older player would have taken the safe way out and simply cleared the ball to the sideboards and lived to play another period.

Heguy made a lightning calculation. With Gracida beaten, only three opponents remained to disrupt him, but they—Trotz and two Piereses— had drawn in to apply maximum pressure. These men, veterans three, were not thinking the unthinkable but doing what they do best, applying pressure, waiting for the other team to break. The strategy would have worked if Heguy had stuck with the textbook.

He was something of a cowboy. He rode a mare named Marcellesa, the best horse in polo. But Marcellesa was into the last seconds of her third period of action. Three periods is a lot for a polo horse at this ultimate championship level; two is usually the maximum. Espadaña must have reasoned that she was tired.

Marcos Heguy aboard Marcellesa pounced on the ball and took it on his mallet and crossed in front of his own goal. Then he began to fly. He galloped all the way over to the opposite sideboards. With the ball gently tucked into his mallet, cupping it in front of him, tapping it along, he started upfield. He had 360 yards to go.

Marcos had the horse; he had the youth and a few extra seconds of total surprise. Near midfield he did something entirely brilliant. He abandoned the sideboards—where eventually he would have been squeezed into expiration by his pursuers—and sliced a shot directly toward the center of the field. In the process he performed a grand trick that maybe a young god can execute when he's riding Pegasus. He shifted the direction of Marcellesa in midair. Instead of galloping along the sideboards, he headed laterally across the field inside his own flow of play.

It wasn't as if he lifted the horse and replanted her at full gallop. There was no "as if" about it; that's what happened. His magic feat required great strength, a great polo player, a great horse. All things concerted.

Heguy did not commit the telling youthful folly. An easy thing would have been for him to move complexly and brilliantly through dangerous traffic inside the yawning mouth of his own goal—and then, galloping all alone at midfield with his enemies a stride behind, make the classic whiff.

From the time he took the ball to the moment of hitting that final backbreaking shot as time expired on the clock, he was pulled with magnetic inevitability.

Above: Gonzalo Heguy in action
Below: Marcos Heguy at left, with
Indios team, 1987

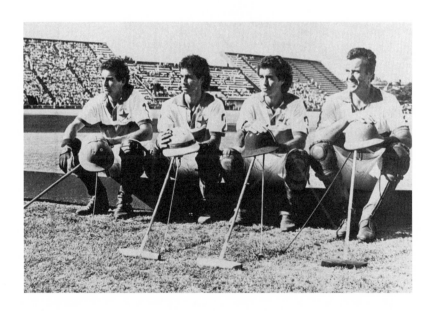

Performing the miraculous was really the only way to beat Espadaña. They had to be sucked into the certainty of victory and then have certainty snatched from them. They would not be beaten on a mistake.

The championship was over in two shots. One from midfield, another brutal long shot from eighty yards out, the ball still rising when it soared between the goalposts.

I WATCHED Gonzalito Pieres and Carlos Gracida on that soft afternoon at Pilarchico, having their lovely moment cantering around the field. Gonzalito receiving gracious, deft passes. The high seriousness of Carlos Gracida. Children like to be treated with high seriousness.

I thought back to that moment a year before when Gracida's horse sat down, and Marcos Heguy started on his way. Carlos was now putting his black horse through speed trials, perhaps to make sure it too didn't sit down and cost him a championship.

Three days later the finals took place. Espadaña against Indios.

Indios had a long-distance, ride-until-exhausted, Pony Express energy. That, combined with youthful and infectious exuberance, incorporated an audience into their every effort.

La Espadaña was a better team than Indios. I had come to see Marcos Heguy's goal as a glorious fluke. In turn my sympathies resided a little with Espadaña. There was nothing to do in the end but stand back and admire them.

INDIOS SHOULD have taken that year of victory, following their coronation as the world's best polo team, and initiated changes. But one year later they had made no adjustments, and their weaknesses glared in the sun.

They wanted to have it both ways. They played with marvelous speed and fluidity, but kept a classic big hitter at defense. If Indios had replaced him with some gaucho kid fresh off the pampas, things might have been different. With four whirling dervishes to contend with instead of three, Espadaña would have had absolute fits.

As the game progressed, Indios's flaw became apparent. In the end it was like watching three different teams—Espadaña, Indios, and this lonesome defensive player with the big shot.

I must explain that the player, a nine-goaler named Alex Garrahan, was superb. Any team would have welcomed him and won with him. American fans would have regarded him as a master. But in this championship he was a Rolls-Royce in a race dominated by Maseratis. A stately classicist. As the game progressed, his long shots increasingly seemed like kickoffs rather than integral contributions to his team.

Alex Garrahan was the first-rank polo player closest in physical stature to a professional athlete. He might have been a tight end in football, or a cleanup hitter in baseball. Big shoulders and forearms, six feet tall, solid muscle. He could hit the ball. He was very pleasing to the crowd, as is always true of power unleashed.

It was one of the best games I've ever seen. The field of the normally beautiful Palermo Stadium was burned out. There had been no rain for weeks. The ball bounced unusually high off the hard surface, making it difficult to hit. This favored close position play, at which Espadaña excelled.

Because Indios played so fast, they were dependent on straight bounces and accurate shooting. Whenever they overran the ball, it took them desperate seconds to regroup. Like power hitters in baseball, they waited for the hard fastball and were easily fooled by a change-up, lunging at it, looking silly.

Paradoxically, the cautionary field surface made the power hitter Alex Garrahan look especially good. By hanging back, he had an extra second or two to set up for his tremendous shots.

I had it firmly in mind to have a close look at Marcellesa, the mare who had been the heroine of the previous year's championship. That winning goal was still what everyone wanted to talk about. Rashomon-like perspectives on the epic moment were proclaimed.

Shortly before the game, I walked across the field to see her. I had built Marcellesa into a giant who gave off her traits so visibly that one simply stood back to look. But she was a small, sleepy, bay-colored mare bunched in among a string of larger horses. Head down and nodding slightly, an orange blanket draped across her withers. A groom wearing a gaucho hat and pantaloons waved her out to me casually, as if she were a mere part of the environment.

Marcellesa looked like a child's pony, displaced from riding ring or fenced meadow. I detected no flash of combat in her eyes, though out on a polo field one could spot her instantly from among seven other horses.

One sees this slow and sleepy attitude in great athletes, as if every common movement were an effort. It has to do with the instinctive conservation of energy. The game was to come, there was no need yet to ascend to anything beyond placidity, so she might as well get her rest.

I had a couple of pats for Marcellesa, couldn't wait to see her in action, observed grooms preparing for the championship to come, laying out tack and mallets. Already one of the Indios players, Garrahan, was up on his horse and heading out to the field for warm-ups. He rode a chestnut and wore a red-and-white-striped jersey, the Indios colors.

There was an accessibility about Indios, an informality about their camp, that was a joy. You could get close to them in more ways than one.

This stood in marked contrast to the pregame encampment of La Espadaña. There, at the opposite end of the field among shade trees, all was efficiency and bustle. Espadaña was the exiled royalty of polo and acted as such. Hurried words were exchanged, messages delivered, autographs deigned; celebrities hovered. Their horses shone; they had a symmetry of efficiency.

This was big business. They were men in the prime of their careers. Their grooms had brisk, assigned tasks, like pit crews.

One always admired Espadaña from afar, as one would admire a piece of engineering finely tuned. Polo was a grim business for them, perhaps because they had had to work themselves up from the bottom in a sport that features so many aristocrats. The Piereses, Gonzalo and Alfonso, had started as grooms.

Indios, having stumbled into eminence, could just as easily stumble out again. Their camp had the aura of a cattle drive, of setting down here at this place for just one game and then loading up the chuck wagon and moving on again. They wanted to win, but what they really wanted to do was ride horseback up and down the field as fast as they could. It struck me how unusual it was in sports to see people having fun.

Marcos Heguy, the team's most prominent player, arrived while I was patting Marcellesa, studying the tack, making notes, snapping pictures. He was a tall, dark-haired man in a sports shirt and white chino pants. He looked jaunty but hung over, as if he'd had a grand night. He had none of the appurtenances of polo. For a minute I thought he must be another, nonplaying member of the Heguy family.

Heguy fell asleep in some bushes. He just sat down, leaned back, and fell asleep. He had arrived five minutes before the players were due out on the field, ten minutes before the Super Bowl.

Sound asleep.

Watching him snooze, I decided he had to be a spectator, since I had no idea where he was going to change out of those chino pants. I didn't see his jersey around, and nobody in the Heguy camp paid any attention to him.

I turned away and searched for the real Marcos Heguy. I wanted to ask him about last year's goal, about Marcellesa, and about his strategy for the upcoming game. His cousins arrived, twin-brother nine-goal dynamos also named Heguy, who formed the heart of Indios. They were soon aboard their horses and heading out to the field for a few minutes of practice before the big match.

I turned around just in time to see Marcos Heguy awaken from his slumber, stretch and yawn, climb out of the bushes. In ten seconds, he had tucked his chino pants into his riding boots, doffed his sports shirt, received a red-and-white jersey labeled with number 1 from a passing groom, picked up a mallet, and was astride a waiting horse and heading out to the field, making jokes all the way, apparently unfamiliar with the cold rush of shit to the heart.

I wanted Indios to win. They had élan; they had the futility of élan; they launched hopeless charges into the barrels of guns.

This was the game in which Carlos Gracida, at number 1 for Espadaña, came into his own as one of the best players in the world. Traditionally, a player at 1 must be adept at flash and speed. It is he who gallops out in front to receive accurate passes from more talented team-mates. Fans respond readily to his breakaway gallops.

Carlos Gracida was more than just flash. His solidity lent his team overwhelming superiority. The game soon became a matter of one great player passing to another great player who passed upfield to another great player—everything performed at a full gallop.

If Espadaña got thrown onto the defensive, their fine back, Ernesto Trotz, reversed the flow of play. That wore the opposition down.

Indios played heroically. They kept coming back in a game that continually threatened to become a rout. They would get four goals behind, rally, take the lead briefly, lose the lead, fall further back, rally again.

The accident waited to happen.

Marcos Heguy flew over his horse's head at full gallop. He landed on the hard turf and lay motionless. His horse rested a hoof daintily, terrifyingly, on his neck. The slightest pressure from that half ton of animal, mere gentle pawing against jugular vein or carotid artery, would have killed him.

The horse's inadvertent placement of hoof lasted for the longest time. As a polite afterthought, the horse finally removed it from Marcos's neck. Marcos rolled gently away but stayed on the ground facing the sun.

An ambulance, a green Chevrolet van, pulled up in front of Heguy. He sat up groggily, waved away a proffered bandage. Falling off a horse at high speed, with all one's concentration on racing to the ball, is a huge shock—flung like a doll, spattered on the ground. No matter how welded to the saddle he may look, a polo player is only as secure as the next planting of his horse's legs.

This was a three-ambulance game. Most matches in Argentina, in-

Alberto Heguy, second from right,
with Indios team, 1981

cluding championships, require at least two ambulances. I have seen four-ambulance games, in which all four vehicles were put to use, carting players off and carting them back.

Four-ambulance games usually involve intrafamily polo warfare. Among the many large polo broods in Argentina, Proustian familial jealousies build up through the years and through the seasons. Players remember old hits, carry everlasting grudges.

Among kinfolk, the atmosphere is fierce and intensely private. These players have no need to perform in front of fifteen thousand at the Palermo Stadium. Find them a level pampas field in the middle of nowhere, and four ambulances would still be required to take care of the bodies. A private field might also be easier on wives and girlfriends. Perched on their high heels, they wouldn't have to totter down from the grandstand to tend to their wounded menfolk.

Indios was composed of three Heguys and Alex Garrahan. To get into the finals against Espadaña, they often had to beat another team also composed of Heguys. Sometimes Indios played best against family members in the semifinals and did not have quite enough left over for the championship game.

Marcos Heguy's fall was the last gasp for Indios. He got up, refused the cartage of ambulance, and remounted his horse. He wasn't the same after that, and his team wasn't the same. They could have brought in a substitute—every team has one—but Marcos wasn't about to leave the field as long as he could ride.

Indios lost by one goal, 13–12. It was a long goal, unattainable; they might as easily have had to make up ten.

A polo field is so large that it borders on infinite space, descending from field to meadow to pampas and so on, into the distance of one's imagination. It is large enough for a battlefield, spacious enough for cavalry to maneuver. The great marches downfield can seem to take forever when one's team is losing.

By the end Indios certainly didn't have the stuffing in them to repeat the miracle of the previous year's championship.

At the presentation ceremonies, instead of hangdog looks and excuses blabbed into the microphone, the Indios players looked thrilled. They bounced around on the platform, greeted friends and family, blew kisses to the crowd, signed autographs.

A final cliché hit me very hard. I certainly never expected the word to reach my lips as applied to a sports event.

Participate.

They were just glad to be there. They didn't act like professionals, didn't have game faces.

Participate.

In 1990 Indios and La Espadaña refused to play each other. The reasons are obscure but have much to do with intricate Argentinean polo politics, charges of favoritism, family loyalties, and rivalries going back fifty years and more. Indios withdrew from the tournament altogether. La Espadaña played a lesser team in the finals and won handily.

Perhaps it is just as well that they demurred. Polo is based on an unspoken agreement about sportsmanship. Without it, the game turns barbaric.

Even by 1989, so great was their animosity that Indios and La Espadaña players refused to shake hands after games. In the 1989 finals, Espadaña won by one goal, but the game was savage, and three horses died on the field. Removing the sport and sportsmanship from the event raises questions about cruelty to animals.

In 1991 a reconstituted Indios team played a close match with La Es-padaña. The game was so rough that afterward Gonzalo Pieres retired in victory from championship polo. Clearly, the sport had reached its outer limits of speed and danger. Pieres declared, "I don't want to die on a polo field."

It is interesting that two of the best polo players in history—Juan Carlos Harriott and Gonzalo Pieres—were able to express themselves so simply and concisely about love and death.

A polo player must love his horse.

I don't want to die on a polo field.

Both men had taken the sport to its furthest edge, peered into the abyss, and seen the cold resemblance to warfare. The courage is to just climb on one's horse and ride away. Anybody can die or get old, but it takes a sportsman to retire.

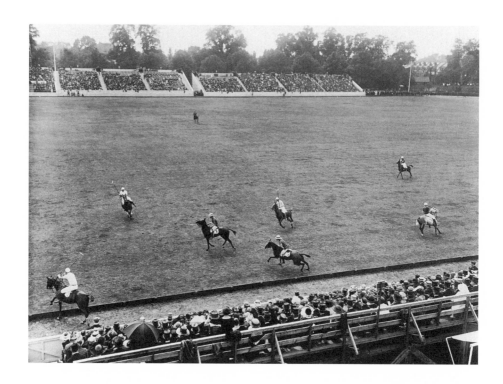

Players near the sideboards at Hurlingham,
1921

Chapter Eight

THE SPREAD of modern polo across the United States can be traced to one pivotal moment in the game's history. That is the August 1933 East-West championship held at the Owentsia Club outside of Chicago, won by the West.

These best-two-out-of-three matches marked the first time that western polo—the California and Texas variety, particularly—achieved national recognition, even though both states had been fielding excellent teams for nearly forty years. Now the best western players appeared together on the national stage to take on the cream of the East.

The teams are worth remembering and so are the crowds—twenty thousand for each game. Special trains brought out eastern rooters to neutral Chicago.

EAST
1. Michael Phipps
2. Tommy Hitchcock
3. Winston Guest
4. Raymond Guest

Michael Phipps was a tough guy and one of the best number 1's ever to play the game. Hitchcock was Hitchcock. Winston Guest was the top indoor player in history and a terrific international competitor, though he never reached a handicap of ten goals outdoors. Raymond Guest, Winston's brother, was outstanding at the back position.

WEST

1. Aidan Roark
2. Elmer Boeseke
3. Cecil Smith
4. Rube Williams

The westerners were big, strong, and rugged. The heart of the team was Boeseke and Smith. Boeseke was a great California ten-goaler and the man who ended my grandfather's high-goal career by sending him spinning into the ground.

There will always be a special place in the annals of polo for Cecil Smith. He was a cowboy by trade, a horse breaker and trainer, and a man who took care of and loved his horses. The great Indian poloist, Rao Rajah Hanut Singh, said of Smith, "I have never seen a man spend more time taking care of his ponies. . . . [It] was one thing which made him a great player." In this he reminds me of the Argentinean Juan Carlos Harriott. One doesn't see so much of this care in contemporary polo.

The earliest polo memory that I have is of Cecil Smith, when I was about four years old. It was a game at the Meadow Brook Club in Westbury—soon to be a housing development and then resurrected on a different site. Ghostly wooden stands from another world, chipped paint, crumbling wood, rose from the perfect field. Smith rode at full gallop, wore a dark-blue jersey, dark-green helmet, and exotic cowboy boots that delighted me, because I always knew that polo was western anyway. All the colors emphasized the snowy whiteness of his breeches.

What struck me as odd about him was that he rode sitting way back in the saddle and leaned back with his mallet extended behind him. At full gallop he seemed particularly vulnerable. I thought that he must have enormous confidence in his horse. I had never seen a man ride like that, fresh from the rodeo, waving almost, as the bright-colored bronc chewed up the ground in front of him. Most of the eastern players rode well forward, and they weren't perpetually poised for a shot, the mallet waiting above like a scythe. Smith was a big man, and he played a big game. He was different from the other players.

I still can't figure out why Cecil Smith is my earliest memory. Perhaps because in frame he reminded me of my father. Perhaps because he disregarded his own safety. Perhaps because I had cowboy movies on my mind, and he was their embodiment. Perhaps because he didn't play the game like a gentleman, with restrained enthusiasm. He hung out there, so to speak.

In fact, Cecil Smith's bravura method of riding prevents him in my estimation from being on a par with the four greatest of all players: Hitchcock, Cheape, Harriott, Watson. Because of his planted rodeo-bronco way of riding, he opened himself for the big fall, and he took many of those falls in major championships. I have the image of an ambulance waiting on the grass near his splayed cowboy boots.

Still, if I were permitted to select an alternate for my all-star dream team, it would be Cecil Smith. He could play any position, hit the ball from any angle, ride like the proverbial wind, and he also had, despite his falls, the art of longevity, which is equivalent in importance to the art of showing up. He was the best polo player in the world for twenty-five years. Something else—he was and is a gentleman in the best sense; more gentlemanly than a lot of eastern pretenders who couldn't hold his boots.

Not long ago *Polo* magazine reported on Cecil Smith's happy retirement in Llano, Texas. He is polo's patriarch now, sitting in the shade, sipping lemonade, watching a couple of good old Texas teams go at it—maybe actor Tommy Lee Jones's four. A class act.

For a description of the East-West match of 1933, I have relied on Nelson Aldrich's indispensable book *Tommy Hitchcock: An American Hero.*

From the opening game, which the West won 15–11, the easterners realized they were thoroughly overmatched. Only Winston Guest could equal the westerners in size. The West team also had a great deal of experience in high-goal polo. Boeseke, for example, had been playing at the top levels for nearly as long as Hitchcock.

The first match was astonishingly violent and a taste of things to come. Cecil Smith was concussed when his horse toppled onto him. He spent thirty minutes on the ground beside an ambulance. A wielded mallet smashed Rube Williams in the ribs, but in fifteen minutes he was ready to play some more.

The second game is worth recounting in full from *The New York Times* account of the action. The dry flavor of violence comes through. In this game Michael Phipps was replaced by Earle Hopping. Winston Guest played at 1, Hopping at 2, Hitchcock at 3, and Raymond Guest at back.

Lake Forest, Illinois. August 16, 1933.

FIRST PERIOD

The East scored quickly on a foul by Williams. Hitchcock took the ball on the throw-in and as Raymond Guest was about to shoot, Williams rode across him. Hitchcock converted from the 40-yard line. Winston Guest and Hitchcock staged a drive from the next throw-in and outrode Smith and Williams, with Guest scoring. Another play of the same kind gave the East its third goal. Hitchcock's mount stumbled, and he was thrown, but was able to resume after a five-minute delay. A

No. 1 penalty on Hopping, who rode Boeseke down, causing the latter's mount to fall, gave the West its first goal. Score—East 3, West 1.

SECOND PERIOD

The Westerners rallied in this period, but wild hitting kept them from setting up a lead. They scored twice to once for the East, on pretty plays by Smith and Williams, the latter following his own long drive from the end zone and outriding Hitchcock and Raymond Guest to tally. Hitchcock scored for the East on a quick solo. Score—East 4, West 3.

THIRD PERIOD

Hitchcock took the ball from the throw-in, dribbled to the side and centered it for Hopping, who needed only two swings to score. Hopping missed a pass from Hitchcock in midfield with no one near and Roark picked it up. Score—East 5, West 4.

FOURTH PERIOD

The West tied it up at the start of the fourth on a foul shot by Smith, the foul being on Hitchcock, who crossed Smith. Williams, trying to get away alone, missed, and Raymond Guest dribbled in to score. Hitchcock gave the East another, converting on a foul by Roark, but the West got one when Boeseke intercepted Hitchcock's pass to Hopping and rode in alone to score. Score—East 7, West 6.

FIFTH PERIOD

Each team scored in the fifth period, with Hopping executing the longest successful shot of the series. He picked up the ball from scrimmage at midfield, dribbled for position and his booming drive rolled through. The West pulled up again when Smith, taking the ball from the throw-in, passed to Roark, who tallied. Score—East 8, West 7.

SIXTH PERIOD

Putting on more pressure, the East stretched its lead to three goals. Hitchcock beat Williams to the ball and outrode him to score. Roark got loose, but missed an easy shot, and the Guest brothers staged a drive. Raymond went up and when Smith rode him out, Winston galloped in to take charge, scoring easily. Score—East 10, West 7.

SEVENTH PERIOD

The West lost Williams in this period and dropped another goal further back. A few seconds after play started Hopping followed Hitchcock up the field. The Eastern leader left the ball to ride out Williams and Hopping scored. As play resumed, Williams was thrown and was taken from the field with a fractured right leg. Score—East 11, West 7.

EIGHTH PERIOD

The Westerners rallied again in a final drive, but the best they could do was break even. Winston Guest followed Hitchcock in and scored, and a moment later Boeseke with Roark and Smith helping him, rode through for the final goal of the match. Final score—East 12, West 8.

Commenting on this landmark game, Nelson Aldrich wrote in his book: "There was more to it than this, of course. Williams, accident-prone to begin with (besides the battered ribs he had sustained in the first game, he had also collided with a goalpost and badly twisted his neck), was out of the series and never again achieved the eminence of national or international polo. Boeseke's fall in the first period was also serious: X-rays later showed that his foot was broken. Nevertheless, he played the next Saturday, his foot so swollen that he had to play in a tennis shoe.

"But it was the sentence [in *The New York Times*] about Hitchcock's being thrown that left out almost everything. True, the horse stumbled, but only after she had been smashed into by Elmer Boeseke's horse. Moreover, she stumbled and fell on Hitchcock's right leg, twisting it painfully. Finally, the delay lasted not five minutes but twenty, while the Eastern captain was totally unconscious."

In fact, Hitchcock had suffered a severe concussion that for the next few days resulted in mood swings from uncharacteristic garrulousness to complete withdrawal. In the third game of the 1933 championship, comments Aldrich, "he was as aggressive as ever, riding out the opposition, pressing the battle without let-up; but his game was off. The anticipation was not there. He missed the ball too often. His passes sometimes went wild—or right to the opposition. He failed to score. In the end he was gray with fatigue, barely able to rise to the ceremonies required of the defeated.

"The [East-West] series was hailed by polo officialdom as having 'done more to advance polo than any single factor since the introduction of the game in the U.S.' " Unfortunately, Hitchcock could not remember anything of the game. His injury resulted in a new rule by the Polo Association: Any player unconscious for more than a minute may not continue to play.

But "advance polo" the 1933 East-West matches certainly did, and their influence has lingered to this day. They made polo a more national sport.

Polo never will enjoy wide popularity. Still, it is played in nearly every large metropolitan area in the United States, whether indoors— nowadays known as arena polo—or outdoors; whether on grass or dirt or on so-called skin fields, where a spray of oil is laid down to prevent unsettling dust from obscuring the players' view and choking man and horse. Skin fields are mainly employed in the southwestern United States, where the climate is dry and summers especially hot. Many of the best poloists from the Southwest spent their youths on dusty dirt fields, not seeing a patch of grass until well into adulthood, when high handicaps made them valuable in the larger polo centers.

Now there is even snow polo, and a snow-polo championship is held every year at St. Moritz. There is ponderous pachyderm polo in Nepal; and bicycle polo informally all over the place. I have seen a photograph, taken in the early 1960s, of Prince Philip with a visage that could only be described as gleeful, pedaling furiously after a ball, chased pneumatically by an Australian ten-goaler named Sinclair Hill, both men wielding sawed-off mallets. I like to think of Prince Philip as having a trusty old Schwinn wheeled from the stable for high-goal bicycle matches.

Television's "ABC's Wide World of Sports" once showed a game that is probably called motorcycle polo. The object is to hit, guide, or bump a giant ball toward a fixed goal while steering a heavy motorcycle. This sport is played in mud, rocks, and dirt by players who are coated with guck five minutes after the opening roll-in. Much time is wasted cleaning goggles. The game has not caught on worldwide; its popularity is focused in and around the suburbs of Ulan Bator, in central Mongolia.

Anyone of any size or shape can play polo, provided he or she knows how to ride and possesses a trace of hand-to-eye coordination. Several women compete with the best. In England Claire Tomlinson is ranked at four goals and has no trouble holding her own in the toughest company. In America there is Sunny Hale, a three-goaler (the only woman ever to achieve this rank from the United States Polo Association) who has played against first-rate competition. The United States Women's Open began in the 1990s and is likely to remain an annual event.

If polo continues its incremental increases in popularity and interests more women, the sport will be less liable to economic vagaries. Women can ride just as well as men—we see this at horse shows and point-to-points—and certainly women jockeys can excel against their male counterparts in thoroughbred racing. It is no accident that Mary Bacon was the winningest jockey at the Saratoga race meetings in 1992.

Also, women may have more empathy for horses than men have, and they often bring out the neglected best in a polo pony. Too many males play macho yank and jerk, wherein the horse winds up with a bloody mouth and after a while is no good for polo.

I have seen brutalized horses whose mouths have turned to iron exact revenge against harsh riders by simply not stopping. Enough becomes enough in a uniquely terrifying way. Horses have cantered into fences, climbed clubhouse steps, taken off across polo fields with the rider still aboard, yanking and pulling. The reluctant passenger is faced with a choice—either debark and risk snapping his legs or hang on and wind up in the club's grill room.

A myth about women is that they lack the strength to play the power game, the big-hitting game, the flat-out game of higher handicaps. But hitting a polo ball is a matter of timing. The longest hitter in polo history was Pete Bostwick, an eight-goaler who had been a steeplechase jockey in his youth. In the 1930s a long-ball-hitting contest was held at the Meadow Brook Club. Tommy Hitchcock was there; Cecil Smith was there, as well as the rest of the greats of American polo—guys who could crush the ball. Bostwick won handily because he concentrated a totality of strength on the diamond-cutter's impact of mallet with ball.

I watched Bostwick for many years, because he often played on the same Meadow Brook or Bostwick Field team with my father. His powerful stroke was no fluke; and he might have demonstrated more of it but his great delight was in the galloping chase, not the hitting. He loved to play number 1 because he could fly out in front of the pack. He developed a lovely scooping motion with his mallet that poured the ball forward as if it were not being hit but ladled. He liked to play on short-grass fields, where he could get into this headlong momentum.

I don't know if a woman will ever reach a handicap of nine or ten goals, but it is not impossible. What is needed is more women being allowed to indulge their passion for the game. All the ten-goal men do nothing except play polo every day of the year, and that gives them a tremendous advantage.

I have heard it said that a woman will never excel at polo at the higher handicaps because women can't handle the rough and tumble of a really violent game. The close-in work of horse and rider. This is nonsense. Too many high-goal male players show off by using their bodies to move an opponent off the ball. This looks good from the grandstand—antic pushing and shoving, back and forth at full gallop down the field—but it is bad polo. Why use your body to ride off an opponent, risking a penalty, when you are aboard a half ton of animal that can do the work more efficiently? I have seen ten-goalers flail their elbows and shoulders for a hundred yards and more; they should know the drill by now.

The problem with polo in this country, and around the world for that matter, is that its roots are wide but not deep. The roots do not nurture, and they are subject at all times to economic considerations. Playing at the low-goal amateur level does not require a great deal of money, but it does require some—though certainly not in the million-dollar range of the grand patrons.

But what is most pleasurable is that the game is countrywide. It is no longer played just on the East Coast—just at Myopia, for example, which recently celebrated its centennial as a polo capital; or Meadow Brook or Palm Beach. There are games everywhere, from Hawaii to Toronto, and college programs have continued to be popular. While polo is played well in traditional eastern bastions like Yale, Cornell, and Virginia, there are newcomers now, such as Colorado State and University of California, Davis, who give the Old Guard a run for their money. Arizona State fields a good team and recently won the NCAA championship, beating off the threats of eastern rivals.

. . .

IF IT WERE up to Eileen Bartolino, the manager and coach of Yale University's polo and equestrian teams, polo would be our national pastime.

Five feet two inches tall, forty-four years old, Bartolino's epiphany came at a game in Palm Beach several years ago. Though she had ridden horses all her life, she had never seen a polo game. On this afternoon there was a high-goal match sponsored by Cadillac and Rolex. Bartolino was transfixed by the action.

"I have to play this," she said aloud. It was a vow more to herself than anyone else, sitting there in the grandstand with her friends on a sunny Florida afternoon. There occurred then one of those defining moments in a person's life. Had it not happened, Eileen Bartolino would probably have let the afternoon slide. She already had a full-time job as a cardiovascular emergency-room nurse at Waterbury Hospital in Connecticut, with high-stress days that began at five-thirty in the morning.

"I have to play this."

A well-dressed man—blue blazer, ascot—turned in his seat, looked haughtily at Eileen Bartolino, and declared, "Women do not play polo."

The rest is history. In 1992, she was ranked by the U.S. Polo Association at two goals indoors and zero outdoors. She runs a highly successful community polo program in addition to her Yale duties. For less than the cost of tennis lessons, she will teach anyone in the New Haven community from eight years old to seventy how to play polo. After about ten lessons she puts the novice in a real game against opponents at a similar level.

To hear Eileen Bartolino talk is to feel optimistic about the future of the sport. Far below the high-goal players and the patrons, the car sponsors and the big trophies—away from Palm Beach and Greenwich—there is the game itself.

Speaking as a cardiovascular nurse and one acquainted with stress, Eileen Bartolino regards polo at any level as an excellent tension easer: "When a man or woman is riding a half ton of animal and trying to hit a little white ball with a narrow mallet, they simply don't have time to think of anything else. Polo concentrates the mind wonderfully."

This is not the world of thirty-thousand-dollar horses and high-priced Argentineans and shouts of "Leave it!" Almost all of Eileen's students are from the New Haven area, and some are from the city's ghetto.

While Bartolino agrees that skilled women can play polo with anyone, she believes that all novice players get more fun out of the game if they start by playing indoors. There is less sheer acreage to cover, passes and shots don't have to travel two or three hundred yards, and there is much more mixing it up between teams.

Most important, everyone gets into the action. Too much outdoor polo is formless and listless—riders wandering around in the hot sun far away from the grandstand. We are not talking about major-league polo now or wonderful hostilities among ten-goalers, but of the average low-goal outdoor game played on a field that for the exhausted novice can expand endlessly toward the horizon.

Also, indoor polo is spectator-friendly. The crowd is right on top of the action, whereas outdoor spectators quickly become bored because the players are almost always a distant grouping. The spectators turn away—fatally for the sport—and the game is lost to them from that moment on.

Crowds of five thousand have attended indoor games at Yale, and they tend to get pleasantly rowdy. Not a blazer or ascot in sight, just a lot of horse manure and kicked-up dirt, quick gallops and lightning turns. The players show their human faces, and for some spectators that is the beginning of being a fan.

Polo lessons for less than the price of tennis lessons. And it is happening around the country, not just in New Haven, but wherever there is an indoor polo facility and someone with enthusiasm to run the program. What is terrific is when polo loses its stuffy image and becomes a cowboy game. Some eight-year-old kid from the ghetto wheels his horse around and heads upfield. . . .

It makes up for all the pretentious days.

The efforts of people such as Eileen Bartolino have only recently begun to offset the steady decline of polo since the 1930s—a decline determined by many economic and social factors. Wars intervened; money got redistributed; great fortunes broke up. For a modern audience, polo, like soccer, does not televise well because the field is so large. A new age also values individual achievement over the rigors and subtleties of teamwork.

Regrettably, quality has also declined over the years. Since polo is not a statistical sport—and statistics win arguments—this decay is hard to measure. In every statistical sport an athlete of today is markedly better than one of yesterday. Yet each year polo's decline at the Argentine national championships, where the best players gather, is plain to see. Most high-goalers have arrived home from points north, having spent the northern summer with teams of uneven quality.

A month of solid practice among peers is required for the players to get back into championship shape. Even then there are instances of unforgivable sloppiness. Superstars have had to ignore teamwork in order to survive the unique demands of polo among their patrons in the United States, Europe, or Australia.

In the United States these high-goal players rarely hit a backshot, which is to polo what a backhand is to tennis. A high-goal player can't be sure that his less skilled teammates will be in position behind him. The professional must circle the ball until he faces forward with the whole field spread out, a tactic enabling him to locate teammates and opponents. Then he can either pass the ball with confidence or carry it upfield alone, which is doubtless what he prefers, since it gives him perfect control over the play.

At this skewed level, polo is not a team sport, but a matter of individual achievement. If the patron wants to play the game instead of just sponsoring a team, that's his business. Small wonder, though, that small crowds watch polo. No one would pay to see Ted Turner or George Steinbrenner flounder around in center field, at least not more than once.

The real difficulty comes when polo stars attempt to break their bad habits. Argentina is full of hungry young competitors just below the topmost levels. Players who know how to give another athlete problems.

If Carlos Gracida, to take an example, ever tried to turn on a ball in a major championship, he would get run over. Another player would be on top of him before Gracida had finished contemplating such a move. That lovely arc Gracida used so successfully in Greenwich or Palm Beach, that made him look brilliant, worked because lesser players gave someone of Carlos Gracida's caliber a wide berth.

That doesn't work in the championship.

High-goal players must relearn trust in the skills of their teammates and trust in themselves not to restrain a pass, not to anticipate, not to think, "Well, my teammate won't get to it. I'll keep the ball on my mallet and take it upfield."

In a top-level game Gracida would not have the luxury of being dazzling. A nine- or ten-goal opponent would muscle in and take the ball from him. The object of high-goal polo is to stay out of traffic and stretch your teammates across the field. There is hard running all the time. Sometimes horses are changed at midperiod to gain an extra advantage.

What made Marcos Heguy's length-of-the-field goal in the last seconds of the 1987 Argentinean national championships so amazing was that his horse, Marcellesa, was running on empty, yet still had the fortitude to go full out for another fifth of a mile.

High-goal players lead a nomadic existence, and the top teams practice together only a few weeks a year. By contrast, to use a baseball analogy, one infield of the Los Angeles Dodgers played together for a decade, and the players knew one another's moves in their sleep. Nothing like that exists in polo, a game infinitely more dependent on team play than is baseball. The result is bad polo.

My grandfather, Devereux Milburn, thought a lot about polo, wrote essays and books on the subject, had many opinions about how the game and his position should be played. He loved playing with Tommy Hitchcock, the living embodiment of all his polo theories.

Hitchcock must have been a source of great confidence to my grandfather, knowing that the perfect pass could be made to the perfect player. Also Hitchcock played the game with extreme seriousness, elevated it by his seriousness, made it something supreme.

The emperor of games.

RECENTLY I saw a match outside of Geneva, Switzerland, on a sunny field shaped like a teardrop, fringed at the bottom with thick woods. If things had proceeded at more than a canter, someone might have wound up in a tree.

The players were unskilled, but the game was still beautiful in its casualness. The people who wandered over and found the game sat under shade trees with lapfuls of grass before them.

My one-year-old daughter took off at a precarious totter across the field with her arms spread wide and her voice at a pitch of delighted gurgle. Play kindly stopped for her.

A sheepdog tried to herd the horses, dashing around the fringe of field, endeavoring to move them into that corral of teardrop grass near the woods.

I remember as a child that the best fun of polo was the late-afternoon practice games, with nothing at stake. Those summer afternoons.

Next year, said the owner of the field, who lived in a big stone country house nearby, they were going to bring in some six- and seven-goal Frenchmen to improve the level of play, to organize the pickup games, to put some order into the motley scene, make things competitive, get a tournament going. Even though it was late spring, there was still snow on the peaks of the Jura Mountains far away over his shoulder. I said, Why would you want to do that?

Epilogue

O N APRIL 6, 1990, six American ten-goal polo players—three of them still living—were inducted into the newly founded Polo Hall of Fame in Palm Beach, Florida. "It is with distinct pleasure that we honor these great stars," said Philip Iglehart, chairman of the museum. "And it is only fitting that we do so now."

It is worth noting the names of these players and their achievements as described by the museum.

HARRY PAYNE WHITNEY
1872–1930

A thinking man's player, Whitney was "the best polo captain of his day," the heart and soul of America's Big Four. He developed and put into practice a new attacking style of play that enabled the United States to beat the British for the first time in the 1909 Westchester Cup. They, in turn, praised their worthy adversary: "Mr. Whitney realized that if polo had become a game of skill it could be greatly improved by intelligent leading."

His attention to every aspect of the game included a passion for finding, breeding, and conditioning the best horses. He is credited with introducing Thoroughbred blood into the American polo pony stock, and he became a valued consultant to U.S. international teams long after his playing days (which included five years at 10 goals) were over. "His knowledge of the game and his experience make him one of the wisest counselors to whom this country turns for final advice and judgement on all matters of polo," wrote historian Newell Bent in 1920.

DEVEREUX MILBURN

1881–1942

An international star who revolutionized the position of Back, Milburn was admired by all who saw him play. "The greatest player on the field and deserves to be described as the greatest player in the world," the British press wrote almost 80 years ago. He was a member of more Westchester Cup teams than any other U.S. player (seven) and was one-fourth of the famed Big Four, the U.S. team that claimed the Westchester Cup from the British and never lost an international match.

Milburn learned the game as a youngster in Buffalo, New York, and went on to hold a 10-goal rating for 12 years, from 1917 to 1928. Although he retired from international play in 1927, his influence on the game never seemed to diminish. When asked to select his all-time polo team, Tommy Hitchcock had no doubts about his No. 4. "He's in a class by himself. If there were four Milburns, my choice for an all-time team would be Milburn, Milburn, Milburn, and Milburn."

THOMAS HITCHCOCK, JR.

1900–1944

Perhaps the greatest player of all time, Tommy Hitchcock was the beau ideal of the gentleman athlete: talented, handsome and self-effacing. Had his career not been cut short by his death in a fighter-plane crash, who knows how long he would have remained at the pinnacle of the sport? The son of a 10-goal player (Thomas Hitchcock) and a skilled horsewoman (Louise Eustis Hitchcock), Tommy won the U.S. Junior and Senior championships at the age of only 16, became a 10-goaler at 21 and held polo's highest rating for 17 years.

He was, first and foremost, a team player and a natural leader, but also a man of extraordinary individual ability. "He could do things you simply wouldn't believe," said 8-goaler Pete Bostwick. It is said that once when he rode hard into an opponent and caused the man's horse to stumble, Hitchcock grabbed the falling player with his left hand (still holding the reins), pulled him back into the saddle and in the next second hit a tremendous near-side backshot.

"He brought out the best in all of us," said former teammate W. Averell Harriman. "He encouraged us in every way with his excellence."

STEWART IGLEHART

Many say he had the best backhand shot in the game; Stewart Iglehart achieved his 10-goal rating through hard work, discipline and a considerable amount of natural ability—he was an all-star in both polo and ice hockey. Like Hitchcock, he was a player prodigy, beginning his career on the Old Aiken team made up of players 21 and younger. The talented young foursome wrote polo history in capturing 11 tournament victories over a four-year period.

Iglehart was 28 when he achieved his first 10-goal rating in 1937, and remained a 10 for all but one of the next 19 years. "A brilliant and resourceful player," commented *Polo* in 1937, "at his best when the going is hardest." No. 3 was his position, and from there he led five teams to U.S. Open championships, and twice won the coveted Westchester Cup. He retired in 1956—still 10 goals.

CECIL SMITH

No one has owned a 10-goal rating longer than the popular Texan, Cecil Smith. For 26 years, 25 of them consecutive, he held polo's highest rating, delighting crowds with his powerful hitting. He came to true national prominence in the 1933 East-West matches when he and his Western teammates shocked the polo world by defeating the Easterners in two out of three games. "For three games, Cecil Smith was the superlative polo player," Peter Vischer wrote in his account of the series for *Polo* magazine.

When Smith rode onto the scene in the 1920s, he was anything but the prototypical polo player of his day. A "cowboy," they called him; but this cowboy could ride and play circles around most of his well-heeled urban contemporaries. He was a member of five U.S. Open–

winning teams and by the time he reached retirement, he had carved his place for all time in polo history. His son and grandson keep alive the Smith legacy on the field.

ROBERT SKENE

Few players have brought as much style and grace to the polo field as Bob Skene. "Hurricane Bob's" career was remarkable for two reasons: one, his 15-year reign as a U.S. 10-goaler, and two, his return to brilliant form after a nine-year hiatus from polo during and after World War II.

Born in India but raised in New South Wales, Australia, Skene quickly became a rising star on the prewar polo scene. He was selected by the British to play at No. 1 against America in the 1939 Westchester Cup. This three-time winner of the U.S. Open and two-time winner of the Argentine Open later came to America, settling in California, where he is still a mentor to many young players. The Skene style is summed up thusly: "The best points of his game were his uncannily accurate strokes and his ability to control the ball when on the move."

ACCORDING to *Polo* magazine, "the three living inductees—Smith, Skene and Iglehart—were present for the historic ceremonies. . . . The other three men were represented by family members: Hitchcock by three of his children and his widow, Margaret Mellon Hitchcock, Milburn by his son, Devereux Milburn, Jr., and Whitney by his grandson, Leverett Miller, a member of the museum's board."

The master of ceremonies for the evening was the polo-playing actor William Devane. He said, "Tonight we have honored the past by honoring six of polo's best. It would not be too much to hope that the men that our generation enshrines are their equal."

Appendix

THE FOLLOWING comprise my pantheon of players who made polo the glorious game it can be but almost never is. In no particular order, these are the great ones, several of whom never achieved a handicap of ten goals.

Thomas Hitchcock, Jr. (United States)
Juan Carlos Harriott (Argentina)
Elmer Boeseke, Jr. (United States)
Eric Pedley (United States)
Leslie St. Clair Cheape (England)
Devereux Milburn (United States)
Michael Phipps (United States)
Horacio Heguy, Sr. (Argentina)
Harry Payne Whitney (United States)
Cecil Smith (United States)
Rao Rajah Hanut Singh (India)

J. Watson Webb (United States)
John Watson (Ireland)
Elbridge Gerry (United States)
Gonzalo Pieres (Argentina)
Bob Skene (Australia)
Stewart Iglehart (United States)
Alan Corey (United States)
Pete Bostwick (United States)
George Oliver (United States)
Harold Barry (United States)

Acknowledgments

I should like to thank Sonny Mehta and my editor, Ashbel Green, for their consistent and continuing interest in this project. Also, special thanks to Jennifer Bernstein, Mr. Green's assistant, who skilfully brought the book to completion.

I should also like to thank:

in the U.S.

> My parents, Mr. and Mrs. Devereux Milburn
> Mrs. Thomas Le Boutillier
> Peter Orthwein
> Alberto Oliva
> George Dupont
> The Museum of Polo
> *Polo* magazine
> Viki Anderson
> The United States Polo Association
> Don Congdon

in England

> Sheldon and Paul Withers
> Lord Cowdray
> Colonel and Mrs. A. W. Harper

Acknowledgments

Geoffrey Kent
Jorie Kent
Ambassador and Mrs. Samar Sen
Major Ronald Ferguson
Mr. and Mrs. Richard Wormell

in Argentina

Mr. and Mrs. Pedro Vicien
Mr. and Mrs. Mario Luis Piñeiro
Mr. and Mrs. Rogelio Pfirter
Mr. Alec Minanovich
Mr. and Mrs. Paul Jablonski
Mr. Amadeo Riva
Mr. and Mrs. Alfredo Viel Temperley
Mr. and Mrs. Richard Alexander
Mrs. Marta Alberdi
Mr. José Heriberto Duggan
Mr. Francisco Dorignac
Mr. Gonzalo Pieres
Mr. Gonzalo Ganoira
Mr. Alfredo Harnott
Hector and Susan Barrantes
The Asociación Argentina de Polo

and finally my wife, without whose encouragement and assistance
this book would not have been possible.

Index

Page numbers in **boldface** refer to illustrations.

Index

Photographic Credits

page

17	UPI/Bettmann
88	Mike Roberts/Only Horses Picture Agency
108	David Lominska
112	David Lominska